THE 100

GREATEST BUSINESS
IDEAS OF ALL TIME

KEN LANGDON

CAPSTONE

Copyright © Ken Langdon 2003

The right of Ken Langdon to be identified as the author of this book has been
Asserted in accordance with the Copyright, Designs and Patents Act 1988

First published 1999
Second edition 2003
Capstone Publishing Limited (a Wiley Company)
The Atrium
Southern Gate
Chichester
West Sussex
PO19 8SQ
www.wileyeurope.com

Reprinted January 2004

CIP catalogue records for this book are available from the British Library and the
US Library of Congress

ISBN 1 84112 513-X

Typeset in 11/14 pt Plantin by
 Sparks Computer Solution Ltd, Oxford. http://www.sparks.co.uk
Printed and bound in Great Britain by TJ International Ltd, Padstow, Cornwall
This book is printed on acid-free paper responsibly manufactured from sustainable forestry
in which at least two trees are planted for each one used for paper production.

Substantial discounts on bulk quantities of Capstone Books are available to
corporations, professional associations and other organizations. For details
Telephone John Wiley & Sons on (+44-1243-770441), fax (+44-1243-770517)
or email corporate development@wiley.co.uk

To Tony, David and Andrew
with my admiration for their courage and spirit

Contents

Four Greatest Licences to Print Money   23

Five Greatest Ways of Winning in the Stock Market   33

Five Greatest Ways of Getting the Order
(or at Least Your Own Way)   45

Four Greatest Door-to-Door Salesmen   53

Six Greatest Financial Necessities of Business Life   59

Eight Greatest Computer Innovations that Actually Make Life Easier   75

Five Greatest Brands Ever 93

Five Greatest Little Office Helpers 99

Six Greatest Management Thinkers 105

Five Greatest Environments for Producing Money Makers   **123**

Four Greatest Ways (So Far) to Become a Multi-Millionaire on the Internet   **131**

Six Greatest Truths Your Independent Financial Adviser Might Not Have Told You — 141

Three Greatest Natural Discoveries that Drive Businesses — 143

Four Greatest Breakthroughs Made by Advertising — 151

Ten Greatest Ideas that Do Not Fit a Pattern — 157

Acknowledgements

This book owes much to Katherine, Mark and Richard, all of Capstone Publishing, who had the initial idea and gave me loads of support and help.

My thanks to the army of friends and colleagues who made lots of suggestions and gave me loads of pointers. Their names are recorded at the back of the book.

Capstone arranged with Henley Management College that I should have the use of their library. My thanks to the college and to Gail Thomas who was the librarian at the time.

*I*ntroduction

A famous business aphorism has been applied to many companies. It goes 'All their plans were unsuccessful, and all their successes were unplanned.' Planned or un-planned, the ideas in this book have the common factor of 'success', sometimes simple but hugely significant (see the *Biro Idea 57*), sometimes hugely complicated ideas whose physical success did not lead immediately to financial reward (see *Eurotunnel Idea 22*).

Thus our definition of success can be seen as wider than financial gain. Over-whelmingly, however, the famous, occasionally infamous, great business ideas have led to huge financial rewards to innovators (see *Edison Idea 4*) and shareholders (see *Coca-Cola Idea 54*).

Perhaps the trickiest part of the title is the bit that says 'of all time.' There must have been a time before *money Idea 39* was invented – and that, along with interest rates, really enabled almost all of the other ideas to be expressed and compared. To look after this type of business idea, there is a section on great financial ideas that enable business to exist.

When you look at great business ideas you are immediately struck by the fact that, however brilliant they were, almost all of them needed to be sold. New selling ideas are in abundance, from good old door-to-door salespeople, through great sell-ing innovations to the wondrous activities made possible by the Internet. I also include the greatest selling or closing techniques which, proven over the ages, are still the best tips for selling things or just for getting your own way.

Then there is computer technology. This has growth on a logarithmic scale. *Microsoft Idea 50* had a growth rate that is far more dramatic than that of *IBM Idea 92* as they each became dominant in their own area. One could be forgiven for believing that nothing could grow faster than sales of Windows software, but only shortly afterwards comes the *mobile phone Idea 96* whose growth we can still only guess at, but in sheer volume will probably be the fastest ever, for the time being. This last one, the mobile phone, has a well-recognised downside as do a remarkable number of other great ideas. Where this is so, we have recorded it under the heading 'On the other hand.'

In technology as well, we have not forgotten the enablers of technological leaps forward. Windows cannot exist without the 'graphical user interface' (GUI), which was the basic idea.

We have avoided the topics of inventions. We were looking for business ideas, particularly ones that current managers might learn from, so generally speaking there are no inventions *per se*.

This means that we have missed out, for example, the spectacular rise of glasses. There is an Italian fresco of 1352, which is the earliest known representation of spectacles. They were invented in medieval times to correct loss of 'accommodating power,' the change in middle age that makes reading difficult. The earliest, made between 1268 and 1289, were two magnifying glasses with their handles riveted together, which were hand held or balanced on the nose. Concave glasses for short sight arrived in the sixteenth century. Bifocals, for short sight and loss of accommodating power, were invented about 1750 by Benjamin Franklin, the US statesman and scientist. There is no doubt that a lot of people have made a lot of money out of spectacles, but it counts as an invention and will not, therefore, be found in this book.

But of course the way to become really wealthy in business is to take a cut of other people's labour, as any entrepreneur will tell you. How to organise people and motivate them is another area where there have been some great ideas. Nineteenth-century mill owners did it one way, the idea of *Theory X and Theory Y Idea 62* did it another.

In trying to pin down the 100 greatest ideas I also became from time to time more philosophical. *War Idea 72* and *religion Idea 71* must have a mention as two business drivers without equal. Now calling war a great business idea may seem insensitive, but the financial side of them is never far buried and economics plays a huge part in war's planning and outcome. I take no moral position on making money out of war or religion; I just note the opportunities that arise from them. I have drawn the line at slavery, where labour costs are literally minimised, as too close to even the modern day bone to call a great business idea. It still exists in places.

There is a very successful bunch of people who make a lot of money eventually out of doing absolutely nothing. Gamblers and franchise owners come to mind in this regard, and we have looked at lotteries and the stock exchange for clues on joining this particular band of money makers.

Product innovation, bumper stickers and training techniques all find their way into the list, as do *junk bonds Idea 69* and the *South Sea Bubble Idea 70*.

A lot of great business ideas are based on somewhat cynical ideas of giving the public what it wants and outsmarting the competition, but there are some theories of economics and some patient advisers on, for example, pensions matters who genuinely made a positive difference to how we live. There are even some computer-based innovations that really do make life easier and we have included *spreadsheets Idea 48* and *call centres Idea 51* as examples of great ideas that make their owners money and the consumer happier.

We have not restricted ourselves to great ideas that benefit the customer or consumer. Great business ideas usually make money for shareholders; sometimes they benefit the customer as well. Indeed *unit trusts Idea 24* is an example where the benefits of the person offering the service are obvious, but the reasons for people buying the service less easy to demonstrate.

How do you choose 100 ideas out of the millions that have created products, services and profits? The answer is to ask a lot of people, and we have done this. We have spoken to people on both sides of the Atlantic, which has tended to give the ideas a UK/USA bias. We apologise for that and for all our readers' pet ideas that we have missed out. Researching the book has reminded us of the infinite ability of man to think of and implement great ideas, and choosing a hundred is a more or less impossible task. But we have done it, and if you and a number of other people buy the book, who knows – we might have discovered number 101.

One of the main criteria for including ideas was whether or not we can learn a quick and useful lesson from them. Where possible we have tried to draw hints for the future from the great ideas of the past. At the end of many entries, 'Ask yourself' and 'Here comes the twist' are challenges to the modern-day businessperson to expand the original idea into their own environment. This should also ensure that you can claim the book's price on expenses. After all, anyone in business can become a billionaire; it's just a question of implementing a great idea. Go on, prove the old saw wrong, make a plan and then make it successful.

Nine Greatest Selling Innovations

Introduction

Putting the customer first is a modern day cliché. But many great businesses have been successful by taking a different approach to markets and prospects. Sometimes a person's wish to live better makes them do something new (*Edison Idea 4*), sometimes it's an off-the-wall change (*Ann Summers Idea 6*) that adds a whole new market, or you can take what you are doing, make a small change and reap the rewards (*Vodafone Idea 8*). But we start with an idea that does not create a product or a market, it just listens to the customers and takes off.

Idea 1 – 'Making it easy, and cheap, for customers to buy' (Sears)

In 1891 American farmers were grousing. No change there, then. This would have been the non-story of the year had their grouse not been justified, and had Richard Sears not listened to it.

The problem was the prices at the rural stores where country dwellers were bound to shop. Using the example of the wholesale price of flour being half the retail price charged to them in the shops, the farmers formed protest movements to fight these high prices and the various middlemen whom they held responsible.

By chance – I wonder how many of the greatest ideas start from pure chance – Sears, an agent of a railway company, had experimented with buying watches in some numbers and selling them to agents further up the railway line. He had then joined with Alvah Roebuck, a watchmaker, and founded a viable business.

Add to Sears' idea the relatively new nation-wide railway system and post office, and the stage was set for the introduction of mail order. Sears understood the farmers well and was able to attract them with the right products and advertising campaigns as well as, of course, keen prices derived from the bulk buying of many products. To watches and jewellery were added shoes, furniture, china, musical instruments, saddles, firearms, bicycles and many other things that filled the catalogue, which by 1895 went to 532 pages.

Add to Sears' idea the relatively new nation-wide railway system and post office, and the stage was set for the introduction of mail order.

A fast expansion followed with a move to a 40-acre, $5 million mail-order plant on Chicago's west side. With more than 3 million square feet of floor space, this was the largest business building in the world.

Suited to mail order was the innovative technique of using a network or pyramid of people to distribute the catalogue. It is in the annals of company history that in 1905 Sears wrote to the company's best customers in Iowa, asking each of them to distribute catalogues among their friends and relatives. The original customers sent Sears the names of the people they had supplied with the catalogue, and received gifts as premiums for their work.

But Sears' innovation did not stop there. Attention to the market had alerted him to the opportunity, listening to the customers forced the company to experiment and move into other areas. Mail order, when it got big, was hampered by the physical difficulty of filling orders and the organisational problem of getting the right thing to the right person at the right time. The company history includes the story of the customer around the turn of the century who complained: 'For heaven's sake stop sending me sewing machines. Every time I go to the station I find another one there. You have shipped me five already.'

Sears executives worked hard on the logistics of mail order. Every order was given on its arrival a time to be shipped, and managers accepted no excuses for not making this happen. Products and parts had to be in the appropriate bin in the assembly room at the assigned time. They travelled to the room by an intricate system of belts and chutes – perhaps the first automated warehouse.

The success of the new system was measured in improved throughput, nearly ten times the original capacity, and attracted the attention of no less an automator that Henry Ford, who is reported to have studied Sears' assembly line technique.

We have mentioned Richard Sears' skills in writing advertising copy, and this triggered the next piece of innovation into what was now a huge retailing company. The copy had become more and more fanciful and flamboyant – more suited to selling snake oil than a full list of everyday requirements. Once again the executives reacted to the complaints of customers, and decisions on catalogue copy started to favour the factual rather than the fanciful. In the early years of the twentieth century it is probable that Sears himself was becoming less active in the copywriting room; oh, and they dropped patent medicines in 1913, with a banner headline in the catalogue reading 'Why we have discontinued patent medicines.'

So by listening to the market Sears produced the whole mail-order concept, and by paying attention to customer service the assembly line methodology was born. There remained only quality. Once again customer demand was that mail-order goods should be of no less quality than their more expensive rivals in retail shops. The Sears response was the 'watchdog of the catalogue.' They set up the first laboratory in 1911 to suggest minimum standards for a number of products and conduct spot checks on mail-order plants. They also made scientific comparisons between Sears and competitor products. The policy at Sears became an unequivocal money-back guarantee.

If only an entrepreneur could do something about the weather, farmers would have nothing to grouse about.

Ask yourself

How robust is your company against the customer's plea to 'Make it easy for me to buy?'

Idea 2 – Dell deal direct

You must have heard the one about 'If the car industry had developed its products as rapidly as the computer industry over the last 30 years, a Rolls Royce would be capable of breaking the sound barrier, use only a teaspoonful of petrol to go from coast to coast and cost less than a dollar.' I have always worried about this since the aphorism should include the phrase 'and be the size of a matchbox' which would undeniably diminish the car's usefulness. But the sentiment is understandable and the selling innovation behind Dell Computer Corporation is a fine example of the truly incredible rate of progress made by the computer industry.

In 1969 a corporation could buy for $350,000 a computer that would contain a central processing unit with 16 kilobytes of core store, four magnetic tapes, a card reader and a line printer. This machine took up some 60 square metres of fully air-conditioned computer room and was capable of doing a lot less than a laptop nowadays.

So what else did you get for your money? The answer to that is that you got a support team: not just hardware engineers – you paid separately for them – but people who knew your business reasonably well and had access to people who were experts in your industry. This meant that the computer company, like your banker or your accountants, were making a contribution to the strategy and running of your business. Indeed, IBM had made this their unique selling proposition in the early stage of their growth.

The reason the computer companies could do this was that the gross margin on the hardware was between 50 and 60 per cent and the software they gave away with the machine was very limited.

The arrival of the personal computer forced huge changes on both customers and suppliers. Falling margins meant that hardware suppliers needed far greater volumes of sales to make ends meet. Customers too were learning just how much more they could expect computers to do. The suppliers turned to other distribution channels – retailers and resellers who added value with software packages.

By 1984 the relationship between a computer supplier and any of its customers, apart from the very biggest, was through third parties. The next pioneering move belonged to Michael Dell who formed his company in that year.

The aim was to re-establish the supplier/customer link by selling personal computer systems directly to corporate customers. The argument was simple. If you remove retailers and resellers you remove time delays and costs, and most importantly you have a direct link between the supplier and customers' problems and expectations. You order your computer by telephone or on the Internet and you get what you need, no more and no less. It was a hugely successful selling innovation and the company has grown to a turnover of around $31 billion per year.

If you remove retailers and resellers you remove time delays and costs and, most importantly, you have a direct link between the supplier and customers' problems and expectations.

Always willing to change its strategy to meet new market conditions, Dell has by no means stood still. Using expensive premises as owned by Wal-Mart, for example, was discontinued in favour of further concentration on the Internet. The Web medium for sales is now approaching $8 billion per year. This is my estimate starting from a number I got from Dell covering the period to 1999. Orders from the Internet go directly to the factory and the company boasts it can assemble and pack a custom-built PC in less than four hours.

Falling component costs plus its own efficiencies offer Dell yet more ways to expand. At present Dell claims some 60% of the consumer PC market where the price tag is between $2500 and $3000. It has only 1% of the market for PCs below $1500. This is their new target. Relying on its brand name and manufacturing efficiency, it expects to compete well in this arena without suffering a body blow from the squeezed margins, the bugbear of the current players.

The company's intention is to continue to develop its direct to customer business model and calendar 2001 was the first full year in which Dell led the global computer-systems industry, with nearly 14 per cent market share. The company tells us to expect further growth, as it believes that the best days for Dell and the whole industry are still ahead. Dell used a useful comparison to illustrate why this growth is likely to be true.

'In 1982 Intel introduced its 286 chip which was capable of processing 2.66 million instructions per second, or MIPS, at a cloc k speed of 12 million cycles per second, or megahertz. Today's Intel Pentium II processors are capable of considerably more than 600 MIPS at 450 megahertz, and the sharp upward development trend is expected to continue.'

This is true as well. The Pentium 4 now goes at 3 gigahertz, six or seven times the old 450 mentioned in the quote. MIPS are not such a relevant measure nowadays because of the different ways that processors use to obey instructions. Suffice it to say that the speed of development has not faltered. Come on BMW/Rolls Royce, match that.

Ask yourself

- When did you last review the channels through which your products and services get to market?
- Check that your competitors are not introducing new ideas in this area.

Idea 3 – Small is beautiful (Honda)

There are many examples of selling innovation that illustrate the point made in the introduction – lots of plans are unsuccessful and lots of successes unplanned. One such is the strategy taken by Honda in trying to break into the US motorcycle market.

The move to the USA was made at a time when there were severe costs constraints imposed by the parent company at home. For this reason the USA pioneers could not get hold of the generous budget to attack a major new market, which the team felt that it needed. In fact they were so limited that they took a minimal-sized team to Los Angeles and stocked a warehouse with 50 units of each model in the existing Honda range. The other part of the Japan-imposed strategy was that they should concentrate on the top-end bikes with a higher margin and an easier differentiator. (It is said that another reason the president advocated this was that the handlebars of the big bikes were shaped like the eyebrows of Buddha, and this was an omen and a selling feature.)

In the event the big bikes did not sell well, and had mechanical difficulties because of the different usage given to them in America, particularly in distances covered.

Short of ideas and also of money, the team in Los Angeles had to use their own motorbikes to get around, cars being out of the question. President Honda had always wanted to provide people everywhere with an economical form of transportation. For this reason he had designed and built small motorcycles which was the form of transport the team used in the USA.

These bikes, as fate would have it, started to attract attention and some local bicycle retailers enquired whether they could sell them. To begin with the Honda managers kept to the original strategy and declined because they were trying to build a reputation for big bikes. However, in order, it is said, to finance the work they needed to do on their mechanical problems they agreed to sell some of the small ones.

To protect the image they were fostering for 'If it's big bikes it must be Honda' their innovation was to sell the 50 cc ones from outlets other than their traditional ones. This improved the depth and breadth of product distribution. From the opposite of the grand plan was success achieved. According to the Motorcycle Industry Council in Irvine, CA, Honda had a 26 share of the 403,000 units sold in 1998.

Idea 4 – Don't build the product, license the idea (Thomas Edison)

The time it takes a product to go from an idea into production depends very much on the industry in which it lies. The time-to-market of the pharmaceutical business can be ten years or more due to all the testing necessary to gain the acceptance of the regulatory authorities. In the computer industry it is likely to be a lot faster. Marketing people in electronics talk of a product life cycle measured in months rather than years.

However long it takes, the problems and frustrations involved in selling products often seem anathema to the scientist or inventor who had the idea in the first place. At least in one part of his life, Thomas Edison decided that the problems of manufacturing were not at all to his taste, and he left the company premises at Newark to concentrate on the research and development side of the business, which he much preferred.

However long it takes, the problems and frustrations involved in selling products often seem anathema to the scientist or inventor who had the idea in the first place.

In 1876 Edison used the profits of his last invention, the stock ticker, to build an 'invention factory' out in the country in Menlo Park some 25 miles from New York City. This was the first time such a laboratory had been built to pursue not academic research, but practical and commercial inventions.

The building itself was on two floors, with the factory itself above the floor that contained a library, a chemical laboratory and the necessary office space. Over time the site expanded enormously.

The expenditure on equipment was lavish. Edison supplied the best and latest in instruments such as microscopes and machines for measuring light and electricity. He also installed his own electrical power generators driven by a huge steam engine. In fact the factory held all the latest in electrical devices. Edison remained a businessman as well as an inventor and set challenging performance measures. He is said to have told a friend that he expected the factory to come up with a minor invention every ten days, and a 'big thing' every six months.

He made his own contribution, of course, roughing out sketches and draughting ideas. The only person apart from Edison himself who had a share in the profits of the business was his chief draughtsman, Charles Batchelor. The rest of the staff were paid by the hour.

Incidentally, Thomas Edison in some ways behaved like the eccentric genius characterised in cartoons by the mad professor with long wild hair. He was able to catnap and be quickly refreshed, or sleep for periods as long as 36 hours. Prior to the long sleep he could work more than once round the clock.

The invention factory was a very profitable arrangement as the bulk of the profits came from the licensing of patents to companies. This meant that every patented idea that was turned into a product contributed to the profits of the invention factory in direct proportion to the sales of the products. During the six years that Edison was with the factory there were 400 patents produced. In the whole lifetime of the factory the number exceeded 1000.

The selling of the idea rather than the product has been reflected in later years, recently in the USA by Jay Walker the Chief Executive behind *Priceline Idea 73*.

Ask yourself

- Are you involved in the most profitable part of the business you are in?
- Is there some way that others could be found to take over some of the risk in bringing your product or your skills to market?

Idea 5 – Check your mortgage at 3.00 am? Certainly, sir (First Direct)

Customer service and banking are two concepts that do not always go together. The retail banking business has been under constant pressure for some years, as competition erodes lending margins and technology continuously reduces the need for face-to-face transactions. This is an industry more known historically for its conservatism and resistance to change than for welcoming new ideas.

A lecturer in marketing and selling, who was speaking to a group of retail bank managers at Manchester Business School in the early 1980s, found himself fielding statements from the delegates such as 'I would like to make it clear that I did not join the bank to be a salesman', and 'What is all this about stealing customers from the other high-street banks? I know the other managers well, they are first class people and there is plenty of business for everyone.' Well, up to a point, Mr Mainwaring.

The huge change to this attitude has been made, whatever one thinks of banking services, in a remarkably short period of time. Banks have thought the unthinkable, and a leader in this process was First Direct a division of Midland Bank, now a member of the HSBC. First Direct started in 1989 to offer a completely untested and, to the majority of people, completely new idea – telephone banking.

Since 1 October that year, the bank has never closed. It has proved to be a very successful method of making financial transactions. Within ten years, 68% of their 900,000 customers were in the important 25–44 age group and 11,000 new customers joined each month. First Direct has over one million customers and over 55% of those customers are now banking electronically, either by Internet or mobile phone text messaging.

Maybe the boldest part of the move was the setting up of an autonomous banking service, affiliated to another bank but not seeking wholly to offer the new service to existing bank customers. On the contrary, it sought customers who were frustrated with the existing high-street way of doing business. Many such customers had the impression that the branch cashiers took their lunch break at the same time as everyone else who, of course, wanted to do their banking during their lunch hour.

As First Direct's commercial director, Peter Simpson, explained, 'Direct Banking is a simple concept which has had a profound influence, not just in the financial services industry but as the rallying cry for a new kind of retailing which revolves around the needs of the customer – not the supplier.' He could have added that it is also a profitable way for the supplier to do business.

From the original telephone service, First Direct added PC banking in 1998. This is another mutually beneficial move as the customer has no delay in accessing their banking information and First Direct replaces people with technology. The PC offering is very wide. Customers can view and print transactions on their accounts, move money, pay bills, view standing orders and direct debits, send e-mail to the bank and apply for all the other services of the bank such as personal loans.

The non-core services have also been built up. Home and car insurance, share dealing and First Direct shopping offers are all available. This last service exploits the bank's ability to access information and obtain good prices for customers in practically any area. Users of the service can make enquiries of the bank on any topic. Researchers will find any product or service on which information is requested, from holiday and travel information to ideas for birthdays and Christmas gifts.

For the future, First Direct depends on the continuing trend for people to work longer and have less, and therefore more valued, leisure time. This, plus flexibility in work hours and working practices, means that people will be more and more under pressure. First Direct sees this as the driver of its long-term philosophy.

Another revolution in banking practices lies behind the customer interface, and that is the requirement for a totally different type of human resource management with an emphasis on the attractiveness of the workplace.

First Direct currently employs around 3600 people based at three sites – two in Leeds and one in Hamilton, Glasgow. The Banking Representatives (BRs) are the people who first answer the customers' calls, and from them the customer forms the first impression of First Direct. They are organised in a network of teams and there are forums for staff to meet and discuss suggestions and changes. The workplace has to encourage the 24-hour working of predominately female staff, so security, safety, childcare as well as sports and social facilities are an important part of the plan.

However good and efficient telephone banking is, there is still opportunity for the high-street banks to sell to their customers, but the queues at lunchtime for 'personal' bankers, who do not know the customers from a bar of soap, must encourage people to wonder if there is not another way.

If First Direct stands still of course it will rapidly be replaced by other banks coming through. This is particularly true with Internet banking. This offers pretty much all the facilities of a banking hall on your PC in your office or home. You can pay your bills, move money around and so on, once again at any time of the day or month. The banks also reflect the cost-effectiveness of the Internet approach by offering better deals on the Internet. Long-term Internet savings can be as much as 4% higher in their interest rate than their best high-street alternative, and often offer instant access and no penalties as well. Today, for example, you can get 4% on a telephone account and 4.25% on the Internet. Such are the cost savings on offer to the banks for people carrying out their own transactions.

When all is said and done, First Direct and its followers are a huge step for banking mankind who, only 15 years ago, 'did not join the bank to be a salesman.'

Ask yourself

- Are you using the telephone to its maximum extent for customer contact?

Idea 6 – Bringing sex to the living room

Why is it that women talking about sex and, for example, watching male strippers find it absolutely hilarious, whilst men in strip clubs are completely quiet and, a lot of people would say, sad? The movie *The Full Monty*, about a group of unemployed Sheffield steel workers who set up a male stripping group, was a tremendous success and had cinemas all over the world falling about laughing. Whereas the MP and minister Glenda Jackson is complaining about a lap-dancing club opening in her Hampstead constituency. Yes, that's right, Glenda Jackson. You probably remember her railway carriage-dancing in Ken Russell's movie *The Music Lovers* and bed-dancing with Oliver Reed in *Women in Love*.

The Ann Summers lingerie and sex aids shops first opened in 1972. They now have 17 high-street retailers in key cities across the UK, attracting 1.9 million customers. But it was the move into selling the products to women through parties held in prospective customers' homes that earns it a place in this section.

Ann Summers is a family company owned by the brothers Ralph and David Gold. It was David's daughter Jacqueline, however, who came up with the parties idea. At the age of 19, whilst starting at the bottom in her father's firm, Jacqueline recognised a new channel for Ann Summers products when she was at an Avon/Tupperware style party. Not only did the move offer a new channel, it gave a new respectability to the shops and products and encouraged women to think more liberally about sex and sensuality.

It works like this. Someone volunteers to house a party and invite as many of her friends and their friends to attend. There are drinks and games as well as a presentation of the Ann Summers product range and the usual product party invitation to buy. There are 7500 party organisers who do the presentations and more than 2 million ladies attend in a year. In the lead-up to the Christmas period some 4500 parties are held in a week.

I am told that an Ann Summers party is 'brilliant fun' and anyone who has been to one reports spending a lot of the time roaring with laughter. That's all I know about them because men are barred from attending. Quite right too: men would probably make the parties quiet and sad.

'Party spirit, which, at best, is but the madness of many for the gain of a few.'
Alexander Pope (1688–1744)

Idea 7 – A non-trivial marketing campaign

The Trivial Pursuit game was conceived on 15 December 1979, when photo editor Chris Haney got together with sportswriter Scott Abbott over a brand new game of Scrabble. The fact that they kept losing Scrabble tiles meant that it was their eighth brand new game of Scrabble.

Sensing a business opportunity (well, if every household had eight sets of Scrabble), they decided to invent a new game. They were, of course, newspeople by profession, so the theme was current events. The questions all dealt with the 5 Ws – who, what, when, where and why. To begin with they called it 'Trivia Pursuit' until Chris's wife called it 'Trivial Pursuit.' which they preferred.

With somewhat naïve entrepreneurial zeal they formed a company. They persuaded Chris's brother John Haney and his friend Ed Werner to join and borrowed money from everyone they knew. One of the original 34 investors was a copyboy from their newspaper who had to borrow the money from his mum. They collected $40,000, rented an office and paid for some of the help with shares.

Today, people play Trivial Pursuit in 19 different lan-guages – not bad for an idea based on the premise that every household has eight games of Scrabble.

The first 1100 sets cost $75 each to manufacture. They sold them to retailers for $15 a game. These were newspeople, not businessmen, so their misunderstanding of profits led to a rapid understanding of debt.

In 1982 the US game company Selchow and Righter became inter-ested. It hired a PR consultant who sent a direct mail campaign to 1800 of the top buyers at the 1983 New York Toy Fair. And then, for good mea-sure, it was mailed to all kinds of Hollywood stars. The mailshot included a Trivial Pursuit card, often one that had the names of the recipients as the answer or the question.

Word of mouth took over. By late 1983, 3.5 million games had been sold. In 1984, 20 million were sold. Retail sales have now exceeded $1 billion. And Chris, Scott and their partners have become quite familiar with the concept of profits.

Today, people play Trivial Pursuit in 19 different languages – not bad for an idea based on the premise that every household has eight games of Scrabble.

Ask yourself

- Is there some way that you could ginger up your Mailshots with a three-dimensional aid related to, or a part of, your product?

Idea 8 – Pay in advance (Vodaphone)

Up front money is worth more than the stuff you have to invoice and wait for (see *discounted cashflows Idea 43)*. So, proving to consumers that they would be wise to do so is an interesting marketing challenge. The mobile telephone company Vodafone took it on with the service Pay as you Talk, a misnomer really since it is more accurately Pay *before* you Talk.

The product is a telephone handset, charger and battery for a fixed price. Calls and texting charges just get lower. A standard call at the moment is 25 pence for the first three minutes and 5 pence thereafter. The call credit is kept on a card and reduces as you use the telephone. When you are running low you receive a message on the handset warning you to 'top up.' You top up on the Internet, or by telephone or by visiting a Vodafone store.

For people whose children have run up huge telephone bills and, for example, for students who want to keep to a budget, this method of payment prevents any nasty surprises when the bills come in. Since it is soon to be possible to access the Internet from a mobile phone this could enhance the benefits of the service. Everyone remembers some of the bills run up by young surfers on their parents' phones.

And from Vodafone's point of view they are being paid in advance. Probably, just as the mustard company's profits are left on the side of the plate, some of Vodafone's profits will be left on unused cards.

Ask yourself

- When did you last review your terms and conditions for payment?
- Is there any way you could argue for some money up front. Don't forget the managers of many big companies are very interested in the price of what they buy because it comes off their budget, but it may mean nothing to them when your bill is paid.

Idea 9 – Make your friends your customers (Amway)

'The business of America is business', remarked Calvin Coolidge, and the story of Amway and its founders bears this out. Rich DeVos and Jay Van Andel met in high school and found themselves at one with their views on the American dream. They were sure that it was possible, for anyone who put the energy and work in, to own his or her own business and grow it to the size they preferred. They resolved to work together towards their dream when they finished military service.

Their first venture was a drive-in restaurant, but it was after a break to sail in South America that their first real success came when they became independent distributors of Nutrilite vitamins. Their version of the American dream evolved into the realisation that direct person-to-person marketing could build a business fast.

Real growth, they discovered, would come when they attracted others into the selling side of the business. Using the same person-to-person method they recruited distributors for their new company Amway. The Amway Sales and Marketing Plan told future distributors how to start selling and getting their own distributors. To begin with, the main product that these channels sold was a multi-purpose cleaner.

In its first year of business Amway sold more than half a million dollars worth of product. Growth was rapid in all areas, but it is when you look at the ratio of employees to distributors that you see the potential of pushing out to more and more friends and acquaintances to bring them into the distributing fold. By the end of the 1960s they offered 200 products and had 700 employees. The number of distributors in the USA and Canada who were, in the jargon of the company, building Amway businesses had reached 100,000.

The 1970s was a decade of further huge growth starting from an annual turnover of $100 million. It was also at this time that the company finally proved to the FTC that Amway offered a genuine business opportunity and was not involved in 'pyramid selling'.

The product line continued to grow with Nutrilite Dietary Supplements and the Personal Shoppers catalogues allowing further diversification. By the end of the

1970s there were literally millions of distributors, not only in North America but also in Australia, the UK and Hong Kong.

In 1980 the company turnover broke the billion-dollar barrier and more plant was added to keep up with demand. Another new product direction followed with the introduction of the Amway Water Treatment System, distributed in the same way as before.

This is what happens if you would like to become an Amway Water Treatment distributor. You approach, or more likely are approached by, an existing Amway distributor who becomes your 'sponsor'.

The selling is done by the sponsor talking about the success they are enjoying. The sponsor also shows the potential distributor a video which, amongst other things, includes a series of endorsements from as eminent people as will agree to do it. At one point in the UK, the video included an MP's wife with the politician himself in the background. At some point the prospective distributor will be provided with the Amway Business Kit, which contains basic Amway products and literature for use in making sales.

The prospect is then invited to produce his or her first prospect list. The sponsor then goes through the list and probably keeps a copy in case you drop out. The sponsor also helps you to sort your people into good, medium and poor prospects by discussing their income level, lifestyle and so on.

You then place an order for the products you wish to buy and for some stock. You are required to pay for your products immediately but have time to pay for the stock as you, it is to be hoped, sell them. You make money out of your sales to customers and so does your sponsor and his in turn.

Don't forget, this is person-to-person selling and, despite appearances, not pyramid selling. You are supposed to be building a business.

In 1997 Amway had a record year with retail sales of $7 billion. The number of employees worldwide reached 14,000.

Ten Greatest Bumper Sticker Strategies

Introduction

The sobriquet 'bumper sticker strategy' comes from the book by Michel Roberts, *Strategy Pure and Simple: How Winning CEOs Outthink Their Competition*. It gives a title to the concept that every business should be able to summarise, in a few words, its direction, purpose and strategy in a single sentence.

Getting a team to work together towards an agreed common goal is difficult, and the bumper sticker strategy helps with this process. The ones I have picked are at corporate level, but sometimes bumper sticker strategies would be better expressed at lower levels in the business as well.

Here is another use for the bumper sticker strategy. In complex sales campaigns where a lot of people are involved it is helpful for the team leader to express the whole campaign goal and strategy in a single sentence. It helps to brief people and gives them a filter to put their comments through when any member of the team, from technician to managing director, is communicating with the customer.

Suppose an account team is trying to sell a computer facilities management contract to, say, an engineering firm. Further, let us suppose that the bidding supplier is the market leader in the customer's industry in the provision of facilities management. But they are not the existing supplier, this would be a new customer. The team will include technicians, support managers, finance people, other customer references, the top management team of the supplier and so on.

All of these people need to be briefed on how to react during their, possibly very short, meetings with the prospect. A bumper sticker campaign strategy such as 'Come out of the cold' helps to remind the selling team how they are differentiating their bid from the bid of the sitting tenant.

A good bumper sticker strategy holds up well against these questions:

1   Does it show a clear differentiator from the competition?
2   Does it promise something of value to not only the shareholders and employees of the business, but also to existing and potential customers? Can I as a customer see what is in it for me?
3   Is it a slogan or a strategy? Do the core competencies of the business underpin the strategy?
4   Is the business organised in a distinctive way to give it the best chance of carrying out the strategy?
5   Is everyone in the business committed to it?

A bumper strategy that sets the hearts of Board members racing may not work when applied to the storekeeper in a remote location in the western Highlands.

This last one may be impossible. A bumper strategy that sets the hearts of Board members racing may not work when applied to the storekeeper in a remote location in the western Highlands. This is why many companies have a bumper sticker strategy that they publish to the world, while encouraging managers to adapt it to a local requirement.

Here are some bumper sticker strategies which are well on the way to meeting all these criteria.

Idea 10 – 3M

Innovation working for you.

Idea 11 – BMW

The ultimate driving machine.

Idea 12 – Federal Express

Guaranteed overnight delivery.

Idea 13 – Ikea

Stylish furniture at low prices for young families.

Idea 14 – Virgin

Debunk the establishment, business as fun.

Idea 15 – Honda

Greatest engines.

Idea 16 – Body Shop

'Green' cosmetics through franchises.

Idea 17 – Johnson & Johnson

Serve medical community, super-ethical behaviour.

Idea 18 – Southwest Airlines

Convenient and low cost point-to-point flying.

Idea 19 – Volvo

Safe durable cars.

Ask yourself

- What is your corporate bumper sticker strategy?
- Which team in or with which you are working could benefit from a bumper sticker strategy?

---

*F*our *G*reatest *L*icences to *P*rint *M*oney

Introduction

As we see in other parts of this book, a monopoly is a excellent starting point for making a lot of money. Sometimes this monopoly comes as the result of winning a contract in a heavily regulated industry.

The phrase 'a licence to print money' was coined by Lord Thomson, the Canadian entrepreneur and newspaper man. He said it in relation to independent television licenses. It works equally well when the government of the day has brought in *prohibition Idea 21*.

One that you may be surprised to find in this section is *Eurotunnel Idea 22*. The reason for surprise is that the tunnel is famous not for being a licence to print money, but rather the biggest black hole of all time into which shareholders and banks poured money. But we need to think forwards as well as back if we are to spot the greatest ideas of all time. Eurotunnel's time should come. I could not leave out the people who are physically responsible for making money, the *Royal Mint Idea 24*.

But we start with a most recent example of an ancient way of printing money – running a lottery.

Idea 20 – Betting with the odds approximately 14 million to one in your favour.

A game of chance where, usually, each of many people has an equal opportunity of winning the main or subsidiary prizes existed in Roman times. Roman emperors used the drawing of lots to give away property and slaves during festivals.

Italy is credited with inventing the modern version of a lottery in the sixteenth century. The purpose of public lotteries was to provide improved defences of cities, or to aid the poor. The very first public lottery to have paid money as prizes was La Lotto de Firenza. Later, when Italy was united, it hosted the first national lottery.

In the UK, Elizabeth I used lottery money to repair harbours and to finance other public works. The Virginia Company was allowed to hold lotteries to fund its pioneering work in the New World. Interestingly, business people regarded the chances of a lottery fulfilling its purpose as very good. They became in fact the 'first and most certaine' way of raising funds.

It is hard to know how such enterprises as the British Museum and the infrastructure of America would have otherwise been financed.

From the earliest examples of the sixteenth century masses of people have been happy to accept huge odds against winning an almost unimaginable jackpot.

While the state ran a fair competition, there were various ways that private individuals could make money on the side. They would obtain tickets at low prices and sell them on at high mark-ups, and there was a thriving business in insurance bets. Since the state made nothing out of these sidelines, they were cited as part of the reason for banning lotteries after 1830.

Ireland set the pattern for the modern lottery in Europe with the Irish Hospital's Sweepstake. Almost all countries in Europe, North America and Asia have national or state lotteries, the notable exceptions being China and India. Australia is sometimes known as the home of lotteries since it uses them to finance much of its public works.

Against this background the Government of the UK offered a licence to run a national lottery in 1994.

The story of Camelot, the company that runs the National Lottery in the UK, would not fit into a category 'the greatest risk takers of all time.'

From the earliest examples of the sixteenth century, masses of people have been happy to accept huge odds against winning an almost unimaginable jackpot. An awful lot of people will regularly venture a pound or more for the small chance of being able to tell the boss what they think of him.

Camelot won the seven-year licence in May 1994 against seven other bidders. The risks they took were cleverly mitigated in a number of ways. First of all, the shareholders were also the suppliers of products, services and expertise to the consortium. The current shareholders are as follows.

1   Cadbury Schweppes brings marketing and sales support with their extensive knowledge of the UK retailing scene.
2   Royal Mail Enterprises are the largest retailer of National Lottery tickets.
3   De La Rue has the expertise and ability to print the high security materials necessary.
4   Fujitsu Services – at the beginning the Fujitsu subsidiary ICL produced the lottery terminals and did the huge training job. They had to train more than 34,000 retailer staff in 10,000 retailers.
5   Thales Electronics are providers of electronic products and advanced systems.

The figures for the half year to September 2002 make sobering reading for the shareholders. From a sales turnover of some £2.276 billion, down 5.2% overall, half went back to the punters as prize money. 27% went to Good Causes (Camelot always spells Good Causes with capital letters), 12% in tax, 5% to the retailers and approximately 6% covered operating costs. This leaves a modest 1% as the bottom line profit of the business. This modesty is in better perspective when you note that the profit before tax of £17.9 million was all distributed to the shareholders.

Camelot publicity makes much of the fact that they had an awful lot to do in a very short time when the lottery was launched, and that the penalties for being late were heavy. Quite so, but the risk that people would not flock to a well-advertised opportunity to get away from the humdrum of work was historically quite low.

In 2001, against very stiff competition, Camelot won the renewal of their licence to run the National Lottery in a bitter and political campaign. They changed the name of the main draw to Lotto; but at this time they are failing to reverse a sharp decline in their sales. Maybe people are catching on to the real chances of becoming a multi-millionaire and telling their boss where to stuff their job.

Here comes the twist

1 The chance of winning the jackpot is approximately 14 million to one. If you do the lottery, stop it at once.
2 Money invested in a premium bond also has only a remote chance of landing a big win. The chances of winning anything are 15,000 to one for each bond you hold. The interest paid on bonds is about 5% so that, in theory, is what you should earn over the long term if you have a fairly extensive holding. But at the end of the day at least the Government has the grace to give you your pound back, some of which you might care to give directly to charity.

'If by the people you understand the multitude, the hoi polloi, 'tis no matter what they think; they are sometimes in the right. Sometimes in the wrong: their judgement is a mere lottery.'

John Dryden (1631–1700)

Idea 21 – Make my product illegal, please

Regulatory interference in a market can sometimes have the opposite effect from that intended. Such interference can be on the supply side or the demand side. Nowhere did the effect of regulation have such an enormous impact on social as well as business life than in the USA when the Volstead Act (Volstead was the congressman who promoted it) was passed in 1919. This prohibited the manufacture and distribution of alcoholic beverages.

The regulation obviously hit at the supply side, but the demand for alcohol hardly changed. The simple result of this is that the price of alcohol went shooting up, and 'bootleggers' ensured that the manufacture and sale of the illegal liquor was widespread.

The best illustration of the stability of the demand side is the fact that the drivers of prohibition were the evangelical Protestant middle classes who were anti-alien and anti-Roman Catholic. They held sway in the rural areas of the country and were generally opposed to the growth of cities and towns. Their attack on liquor was successful because it was assisted by the rural domination of the state legislatures.

The result of prohibition was that liquor was more or less unknown in these rural areas, while reasonably obtainable in the towns and cities. The people who wanted to drink and lost out were the working classes who could not pay the inflated prices that prohibition had guaranteed.

Successful businessmen in the liquor industry were very successful indeed. Al Capone counted his annual earnings in tens of millions of dollars. There was a downside. The gang wars, which accompanied the distribution of liquor, cost a lot of people their lives. Historians of crime, however, maintain that a stable semi-monopoly was emerging towards the end of the 1920s.

Also emerging at that time was a new attitude in the temperance movement itself. Major supporters of prohibition gradually lost faith in it as they saw the increase in criminal liquor production, the development of the speakeasy and the increased restriction on individual freedom. The Democrats adopted a platform to repeal the prohibition act in the presidential election of 1932, which they won.

Most states immediately repealed their own laws, but some kept on until 1966. Since then liquor control in the USA has remained at local level.

Ask yourself

- Is there any way that your product could improve its margins by the slowing down of supply without any consequent reduction in demand?

Join me in lobbying for the complete prohibition of business books.

Idea 22 – A tunnel vision

Mentioned in every textbook on the subject of investment is the need to look at investment in equities as a long-term play. A lot of newspaper columns remind potential investors that they should put money into the stock exchange with a timespan in mind of at least five years.

In this regard Eurotunnel is the *reductio ad absurdum* that proves the rule. But look at the affairs of the company more closely and as a long-term plan, and its inclusion in the section 'licence to print money' makes more sense. It is true that the 1998 accounts show that the company made an underlying loss of £215 million. The financial restructuring gain, caused by the reduction of the past interest bill, converted this loss into a small profit of £64 million. It is also true that shareholders funds were stated at £1.06 billion while long-term loans stood at £8.29 billion.

The shareholders should have plenty to look forward to, or at least their descendants should.

But, like the pundits say, look at the long term. After all, the debate on whether a fixed link should be built started 200 years before the treaty signed between the UK and France in 1986 made the tunnel possible.

One of the earliest plans came from a French engineer, Albert Favier, who proposed a tunnel for horse-drawn vehicles with an island in the middle to allow for changing horses. If you think the shareholders have a long wait for return, consider the case of Thom de Gamond who worked on a fixed link for some 40 years of his life, culminating in another tunnel plan in 1868. Some progress was made in tunnelling in 1880 until the British Government got cold feet and called it off.

Political opposition remained the stumbling block in the first half of the twentieth century, although some big guns, such as Winston Churchill and Aneurin Bevan, supported it. The need for political support changed in the Thatcher years when a joint study indicated that a two-tunnel scheme was a possibility and tenders were invited for a privately financed fixed link.

It was hard to argue with the international panel of construction industry executives and editors when they named the tunnel as the top construction achievement of the twentieth century. This was against other famous constructions such as the Golden Gate Bridge and the Panama Canal.

The original licence was due to expire in 2042, but extra years were granted and the company has sole rights to charging for use of the tunnel until 2086. Eventually this will be another licence to print money – the opposite of Camelot, which is relatively fast in fast out. The shareholders should have plenty to look forward to, or at least their descendants should. Now that is planning in the long term.

Idea 23 – Making a Mint

There is now only one holder of the licence to print UK coinage, and that is the Royal Mint. This was not always the case. For more than 1500 years from the Iron Age to the Restoration of Charles II, coins were struck by hand. To begin with there were many English 'moneyers' operating in towns and villages across the Kingdom. People laboured in what were little more than blacksmith shops hammering blanks between a pair of dies.

A single mint was set up in 1279 within the Tower of London and operated there until it then moved into purpose-built premises on Tower Hill. The present modern coinage plant was built to start the process of minting coins for decimalisation in the UK in 1971. These premises are in Llantrisant in South Wales.

The Royal Mint now boasts some of the most advanced coining machinery in the world. It works like this:

In the foundry, strips of metal are drawn from large electric furnaces, reduced to the required thickness in a tandem rolling mill and transferred to large blank presses where coin blanks can be punched out at the rate of 10,000 per minute.

The blanks are softened and cleaned in the Annealing and Pickling Plant before the final process in the Coining Press Room. Here the blanks are fed into coining presses where the obverse and reverse designs, as well as the milling edge, are stamped onto the blank simultaneously.

The latest presses can each strike more than 600 coins per minute to a standard of accuracy imposed by law. To ensure that the composition of the alloy is correct, samples of the molten metal are routinely checked by X-ray fluorescence spectrometry. Each year samples of coins struck both for the UK and overseas are presented to the annual Trial of the Pyx where they go through rigorous quality examination by the Worshipful Company of Goldsmiths.

The number of coins in circulation in the UK exceeds 18 billion coins with a face value of £2 billion.

In 1975 the Mint was established as a Government Trading Fund, operationally very similar to a government-owned company. For many years half its sales have gone abroad. This role as an exporter was emphasised when it became an Executive Agency, providing it with greater freedom to develop its business further. The Royal Mint has maintained its position as the world's leading exporting mint. During 1995–96 the Royal Mint produced coins and blanks for 82 countries, from Albania to Zimbabwe.

The Royal Mint can satisfy any requirement of a country for a complete range of coinage. To ensure the uniqueness of any coin in any country, the Royal Mint houses, on behalf of all the world's mints, the Coin Registration Office. This enables advice to be given to countries considering new coins so that they can avoid specifications identical to existing coins in other countries. The Royal Mint also maintains close contact with the vending industry worldwide and continuously increases the range of security features that it can offer to discourage counterfeiting.

Of all the distinguished people to have served the Royal Mint perhaps the most unexpected and highest ranked is Isaac Newton. The scientist had a 30-year association with the Mint as Warden and then Master. He took a lot of interest in the Mint despite being informed on his appointment that it should not take up too much of his time. In fact the Government wanted the Mint to provide Newton with an income that still left him relatively free to pursue what they regarded as more important matters.

Newton became heavily involved in the dramatic increase in production occasioned by the great silver recoinage of 1696–98. He was actively involved in the setting up of five mints elsewhere in the country.

But mainly his Warden's duties were concerned with the protection of the coinage from clippers and counterfeiters. This drew him into the underworld, where his usual zeal turned him into a doughty and persistent opponent of such as the infamous William Chaloner, who paid for his forgery on the gallows.

As the Master he was more responsible for the production of coins, where his desire for accuracy kept variations in the weight of new coins within very small tolerances. It must have been a brave Company of Goldsmiths who challenged the composition of the sample coins in 1710. It was particularly brave since it turned out not to be true.

His name lent huge prestige to the Royal Mint and his advice was sought by many. It was even sought by the Scots during the recoinage of the old Scots money in 1707 caused by the Union of the Crowns.

Newton's contribution to the Mint was not so much in innovation or change, but much more in the integrity and scientific accuracy of production. This legacy is maintained to this day, and the reputation of the Royal Mint is still held very high.

'And these I do not sell for gold,
Or coin of silvery shine,
But for a copper halfpenny,
And that will purchase nine.'

Lewis Carroll (1832–1898)

Ask yourself

• Who holds the licence to print money in your industry? Are they vulnerable?

*F*ive *G*reatest *W*ays of *W*inning in the *S*tock *M*arket

Introduction

I recently read the brochure of an insurance company selling a with profits policy. They were claiming, as they all do, that on past performance they were the natural choice. They chose to demonstrate this by looking at the value of policies over a period of time. The period they had chosen was seven years and two months that ended some time ago. It was obvious that they chose this particular period because it illustrated the point they wished to make. It also makes the point that any system for investing, from throwing darts at the *Financial Times* to the most complicated computerised chart research, will probably succeed for some interval of time.

There are periods when Jim Slater's Zulu principle brings home the bacon, other times when it does not perform. With this is mind, we have chosen two investment methods that have some rationale behind them as being as good as any (*dealing when the directors do Idea 27* and *choosing the worst performing unit trusts from a management stable Idea 28*). You should also remember that neither the publisher nor I are licensed to give investment advice – so don't sue if it all goes wrong.

The *investment club Idea 25* route also has a lot of logic behind it but is more likely to produce steady gains over a long period of time than spectacular ones from inspired trading. If that is not fast enough for you, then the section on *hedging Idea 26* shows how a sensible idea can be made to win or lose a lot of money in a very short period of time. But we must start with the people who regularly and consistently make money out of the stock market – the people in the City itself.

Idea 24 – Greatest ways of winning in the stock market? Run a unit trust

I suppose there is no such thing in the stock market as a guaranteed winner, but it's hard to believe that managing a unit trust is not just that. The concept is simple. Although unit trust managers would rarely put it like this, their great business idea is that you give them your money to invest in equities, and they will take 5 or 6% of it before they start investing and then each year 1.5% of the value of the investment *no matter how successful* the investment proves to be. If they double your money in a year they take their 1.5% and if they halve it they do the same.

If using a unit trust reduces the risk of having too many eggs in the same basket for investors, If using a unit trust reduces the risk of having too many eggs in the same basket for investors, then how much more is the risk reduced for the fund managers who develop a range of unit trusts?

then how much more is the risk reduced for the fund managers who develop a range of unit trusts? Look at it this way. A well-known con in racing is for someone, apparently in the know, to sell tips for a fixed price plus a percentage of any winnings. The fixed price is the tipster's guarantee, while the punter will in any case tend to pay the percentage of a win in order to stay on the oracle's books. Oracle is certainly the right word if the tipster is actually tipping every runner to someone and therefore always has a winner to advertise to new punters. You would never fall for that, would you?

And yet the concept that unit trust managers bring to customers is remarkably similar. They offer a multiplicity of trusts in this country and abroad, growth and income, separate industry sectors, emerging markets and so on. The chances have got to be pretty good that at any moment in time the unit trust manager will be able to point to at least one of his trusts that is performing well. This draws in more money and the managers take their 5% up front and 1.5% per annum. It's brilliant.

It's not so brilliant for the investor. It is true that a unit trust spreads small investors' risk. They are able to buy into a spread of shares, which is difficult to do if they are only investing small amounts, and the opportunity to get easily into foreign shares is a definite advantage over doing it yourself. The second main argument usually put forward for unit trusts is more questionable. The managers will claim that they are experts in picking shares that are going to perform well. They certainly need to be to earn their money so let's see how well they have to do.

Looking at what has happened over the last five years of the bull market to £1000 invested in the average unit trust you will find that, at 1999 prices, it had risen to £1580. This is a compound rate of return of just under 9.6%. Could the private investor have done better? If you take into account that the FTSE All Share index, an index of capital growth without taking account of dividend income, did over 16% per annum over the same period you should be able to take a view.

Of course the investor could have been lucky and chosen the best performer who managed an incredible £4278 – or something over 33% per annum. But they could have picked the other end of the spectrum and lost more than half the original stake.

According to the Association of Unit Trusts the value of funds invested in unit trusts went up between April 1998 and March 1999 from £170 billion to £192 billion. The managers' initial charges that year at say 5% gave them £1.1 billion and their annual 1.5% cost investors £330 million. Of course they have their expenses to find out of that, but arguably they have very little risk.

That describes the good times when people were investing in unit trusts in a long bull market. March 1999 saw the start of what now looks like an equally long bear market, and investors are seeing the value of their funds and pensions diminishing very rapidly – over three and a half years at the time of writing. Again, it does seem to be a heads-you-lose, tails-the-unit-trust-manager-wins situation, since most unit trusts are losing much more money than the general stock market. They are simply not appearing to be the hedge or buffer against hard times that they boasted of in the past. And they still draw their initial fees and annual charges – great idea or what?

Here comes the twist

- Read the next great idea.
- Form or join an investment club.

Idea 25 – Run a private unit trust – an investment club

So, if being a *unit trust* manager is such a clever way of making money, how can private individuals get the same or a similar opportunity?

The one advantage of unit trusts over doing your own investing as an individual is that a unit trust gives you instant access to the widely spread portfolio that the unit trust manager has established. If your resources are limited this can be very useful, as it avoids the overexposure to a small number of shares in the early years of a portfolio.

In passing it is worth noting the number of people who hold shares only in their own company. This is the opposite of good portfolio management, which recommends that you hold a spread of at least 15 shares, so that if one bit goes wrong it may be balanced by another bit doing well. Not only that, but if you only have shares in your own company, if the share price goes south it could presage your job going west.

Investment clubs offer a neat way of gaining the benefit of a portfolio without losing control of the investment strategy, or paying the fees of the professionals.

I have to declare an interest here. I have been the treasurer of an investment club for its lifetime of five years. It is a steady, some would say boring, club with simple objectives. It is a long-term savings scheme for its members and the benchmark it attempts to beat is the performance of the average unit trust as reported on Saturdays in the *Financial Times*.

The beauty of investment clubs is that they are essentially informal. They have almost no expenses, since none of the people involved in running the club are paid. But this informality must be balanced by a well drawn-up constitution and rules. You may obtain these easily from such organisations as Proshare in the UK or the National Association of Investors Corporation in the USA.

What happens is this. A group of up to 20 people, neighbours, friends, colleagues or members of the same golf club, for example, agree to form an investment club. Some clubs have as few as three or four members. One of the members gets hold of a sample constitution and rules, understands them and writes the first description of the club for other prospective members to read.

During an inaugural meeting a number of significant issues are discussed and decisions made in the following areas:

- *Office bearers.* The club needs a chairman, a secretary and a treasurer. The treasurer is highly significant in the club as he or she will keep the records of the portfolio and all transactions.
- *Number of meetings per year.* Some clubs meet monthly and others less often. It depends on the subscription income and, to some extent, on the social aspects of the club. Some clubs are primarily social and will meet frequently to socialise as well as make investment decisions. Others are more serious in terms of the objectives of the club and the likely level of the fund as it grows. In any case there will be an annual general meeting.
- *How members are elected.* Probably new members will be proposed by existing members and their invitation to join ratified at a monthly meeting.
- *Subscriptions.* The members must decide on the amount of the joining fee, the upper and lower limits of monthly subscription, and upper and lower limits on lump sum investments. I have seen clubs with monthly subscriptions as low as £20. The average for our club is about £95 per month, with the lowest sub £50 and the highest £250.

The rules also need to be clear on how the portfolio is valued for purposes of buying units in the fund, or selling units back in order for a member to realise some or all of his or her holding. Normally this valuation is made on the last day of the month and the price used is the mid-price of each share as quoted in the *Financial Times*.

Members of an investment club need to have a common goal for the building up of the portfolio. Individual reasons for being in the club may be very different, but the investment goal needs to have the support of everyone. It is probably useful to set it fairly wide. Taking that goal into account, individuals can then calculate an appropriate subscription amount.

The investment strategy is the next important step. This should certainly include the level of risk to be taken. The members must agree what proportion of money is to be invested at low, medium and high risk, and what they mean by those risks. Our club is a savings scheme so more than half of the money is invested in FTSE 100 companies.

If some members are less interested in the nitty gritty of investment decisions, they may leave that to others or even to a sub-committee; but the people with the delegated authority to make such decisions will be bound to operate according to the strategy or to go back to the whole membership if they wish to suggest changes.

The members, or the sub-committee, then choose shares in the way that the members have agreed. Some strategies are no cleverer than sticking a pin in the *Financial Times*, or using members' knowledge of their own industries as a guide. Here is a summary of a more logical way of team share choice.

- Using their knowledge and observation they choose a sector for investment.
- Using their strategy and current spread of the portfolio they choose the correct level of risk.
- Using the price/earnings ratio and yield they identify some four or more shares which are in the category defined in the first two steps. They get the annual reports of these companies. They probably action one or two members to do the evaluation work.
- Using published information they discuss the company strategy.
- From the same information they calculate the key business ratios, discuss whether they support the business strategy and possibly compare them with industry averages.
- They finally evaluate whether they believe the managers of the business can carry out the strategy successfully and make a decision.

In five years, 20 of us have built up a fund of £130,000, and, touch wood, we regularly beat the average unit trust over one, three and five years.

If we take the periods to June 6 1999, just as an example, we beat the average unit trust as follows.

Return on £1000 income reinvested	Average unit trust	Belmont Investment Club	Difference
One year	1034	1039	0.5%
Three years	1272	1564	22.96%
Five years	1618	1797	11.06%

We have not been immune to the huge bear market though and the value of our investment has fallen dramatically. Time will tell if we can repeat this competitive performance in hard times as well as good. I suspect we will.

Idea 26 – Hedge your bets

'Here's a farmer that hanged himself on the expectation of plenty.'
Shakespeare, *Macbeth*

You may remember the opening of the book by ex-Salomon trader Michael Lewis called *Liar's Poker*. John Gutfreund, the Salomon Chairman, comes out of his office and offers to bet $1 million on a single game of Liar's Poker with another senior manager. The bet goes 'One hand, one million dollars, no tears.' The 'no tears' is to emphasise that the bet is for real and that the loser will not whinge about his loss. Indeed, get a group of city types together and they will find something to bet on. Wherever there is a degree of uncertainty, for example of supply and demand, someone will take positions on it.

Wherever there is a degree of uncertainty, for example of supply and demand, someone will take positions on it.

The concept of hedging rears its head in the futures markets in which 'bets' are taken on the value of commodities or shares some time in the future. The history of what is now known as the derivatives markets goes back to some very sensible 'insurance policies' being taken out by farmers. If you are dependent on crops that only grow once a year, you are dependent first of all on the vagaries of demand. How much cocoa will the chocolate manufactures buy and use over the next one or two years? There is also risk to supply as it depends on what the weather is going to be like.

Cocoa is a traditional futures market that started trading in 1926. Commodity suppliers sell some or part of their future crops forward. That is, they agree a price and a volume of product with a trader before all the uncertainties become known. The timing in the cocoa market of this is up to 21 months ahead. Farmers can now sleep soundly knowing that a proportion of their income is protected whatever the outcome at harvest time. The great idea is as simple as that.

But, of course, then the complications cut in. Producers have an interest in concealing the true size and condition of their crops. News of impending shortages will drive prices up; the prospect of a bumper harvest will take prices in the opposite direction. Since there is active trading in these futures, the original buyer can sell the contract on at a profit or loss.

Usually producers work out just how much of the crop they want to sell forward so that if there is a shortage and higher prices are available they will be able to take advantage of these for at least some of their produce. The proportion 'hedged' or 'insured' limits the risk to whatever level the producer deems acceptable.

The chocolate manufacturers are also playing a careful game. Their wish is to guarantee a minimum amount of cocoa whilst at the same time trying to achieve the minimum average price they can. They will buy forward only if they think the price is likely to rise.

This is the classic role of the commodities futures market, providing a way of hedging risk due to uncertainty about the supply and demand for basic materials and the pricing consequences that follow.

The great idea of hedging has been expanded to allow futures trading on stocks and shares. In this way an investor can buy call options at a price set at that time for a trade to occur at a fixed time in the future. Either side in this transaction can thus increase the potential reward of a share price rise by using gearing. It works like this.

Suppose you believe, for whatever reason, that the price of shares in Example Company PLC (ECP) is going to rise over the next few months, so you can buy an option in the futures market. Take these numbers as an example.

The share price of ECP is currently 658 pence. You believe that it could rise some 10% over the next three months to 725 and you have £2,000 to invest. In this example I am going to ignore the costs of dealing to keep it simple. Remember every trade you make whether in actual shares or options is accompanied by a cost which will have the affect of reducing the numbers you are about to read.

If you buy shares in ECP and your prediction is correct you will make £200 or 10% in three months, which is not bad. But suppose you want more. You could buy a call option for 31p giving you the right to buy shares at 650p in three months time. Your £2000 buys you about 6450 calls. When the price goes up to 725p you can buy for 650p and sell for 725p at the same time. Your sale profit is 6450 × (725 – 650) or £4837, from which you subtract the original £2000 you paid for the option, leaving a profit of £2837 – more than fourteen times the profit earned in trading in the underlying shares. You have received return on your original capital of an outstanding 140% in three months, a huge reward.

But a huge reward implies a huge risk. If the market goes against your prediction the outcome can be dire. In effect you are buying the shares for 650p, the option price, plus 31p, the price of the option making a total of 681p. If the price is below that you lose. If the price in three months is 665p then your losses are 6450 × 16 or £1032 and you have lost half your money. If the price drops below 650 of course then you have lost the lot. The only people who cannot lose, naturally, are the ones taking commissions on each transaction.

This principal of hedging and speculating can be applied to almost anything in the stock market. You can, for example, hedge or speculate on movements of the main market indices such as the FTSE 100. This means that your portfolio is protected if you were thinking of selling shares at a given point in the future. You can bet on spreads of prices and so it goes on. If you need an insurance policy hedging is a great idea, but if you decide to speculate, be sure you do it with money you can afford to lose. Most financial advisers steer their clients away from speculating in futures because of the huge risks, but as long as you can write the money off when you place the bet its an excellent return if you are lucky. But don't forget what the man said – 'No tears.'

Idea 27 – Dealing when the directors do

I said I would make two suggestions for a winning share strategy and here is the first. It comes without guarantee and involves buying shares when the directors have done so and following their lead also in selling.

It is extraordinary how news announced by companies comes, almost always, after there has been a related move in the price of the shares involved. A simple test of this is to look at what happens on the day a company announces its results. If the results are in the middle of the range predicted by analysts there may be little or no movement. If they are at the top end of predictions the price quite often goes down. The good news was already in the price. The main players knew roughly what was going to happen before the announcement was made.

It is extraordinary how news announced by companies comes, almost always, after there has been a related move in the price of the shares involved.

Knowledge of the health of a company is revealed in a number of ways. The sources that the private investors have at their disposal are dominated by what they read in papers or magazines, or from material such as annual reports, which they can get from the companies themselves.

Without any hint of insider dealing or illegality, such knowledge is basically old hat before the papers are printed. The people in the know, i.e. the City, will have already taken positions on news before private investors have had a sniff.

The people closest to the real situation of the company are, of course, the directors. During certain periods of the financial year they are banned from dealing in the shares in their own company, because their inside knowledge could damage investors without the directors' access to information.

At other times of the year they are permitted to deal and they do. It is easy to find out when this has occurred by reading the financial pages although the timing problems mentioned above do exist. Nevertheless, following directors' dealings is potentially a way of making money in the long term. The rule is, if three or more directors buy shares in their own company then you buy, and if three or more directors sell shares in your portfolio then you should sell.

It has worked in the past and it will almost certainly work in the future. The only problem you are left with is knowing when.

Idea 28 – Backing last year's losers

With all their faults, unit trusts are a very popular way of private investors getting into the stock market. So here is a possible strategy to pick the right unit trust by studying the form. This probably presupposes your agreement with my thinking that choosing unit trusts is something of a lottery.

The main boast of any unit trust provider is that with the skills and knowledge of their management teams they will tend to outperform their sector, index or benchmark. As we have already seen they will then advertise those funds that do actually achieve this result. The ones that have done really badly get no publicity and no advertising budget. But look at the thing from the provider's perspective and an interesting possibility presents itself.

Because marketers need to attract new money, performance has become more and more important. This means that successful fund managers have become superstars on huge salary and bonus packages. They are also very mobile. According to the publication *Successful Personal Investing*, the average time an individual fund manager has responsibility for a fund is 2.5 years. So, impressed by the performance of one trust and determined to invest in that management team, investors, unless they are careful, could be buying the expertise of a team new to the fund, with a poorer track record.

This means that if you want to follow a manager you may have to switch funds or even provider. This is often expensive with the payment of initial charges. But there may be a way of turning this to the investor's advantage.

If a fund is not performing the providers will at some point change the team running the fund. They do not want the fund to bring down their average and place in the league tables for ever. They also do not want to appear for too long in the 'Worst performing funds' sector of Saturday's *Financial Times*. A change of management may be all that is required to pick up performance and do better for their investors.

There is a strategy to operate on this, which is to buy annually the worst performing fund in any fund manager's stable, on the grounds that the management change may occur and the fund will do better during the next 12 months or even be best in stable. At that point you switch and again buy the worst performer. It has worked in the past, from time to time of course.

There is another piece of logic behind this strategy. At present most funds are dual priced. This means that they have a bid and offer price with a spread that includes the initial charge the managers take for managing your money (you remember the basic premise). As well as this there is a cancellation price. This is the lowest price the management group is allowed to buy back units from you according to the official price calculation. When the bid price is at or near this, the unit is said to be on a bid basis.

This cancellation price is a useful guide to the current popularity of individual funds. If the cancellation price is below the bid price, the price at which the managers will buy back your units, then it is a reasonable conclusion that more units are being bought by investors than sold. The price is known as on an offer basis. It also means that there is scope for a widening of the offer to bid price when the fund becomes less popular.

What you want to do is to buy when the price is on a bid basis, and sell when it has moved to an offer basis. This is more likely to happen if you buy the worst performing fund in a stable.

There is a problem. I said that knowing the cancellation price was useful to the investor, so it is no surprise to find that the rules have been changed. Up until 1995 unit trusts were required to publish their cancellation prices each day. Now they are not, but if you request the information from them they must tell you.

Five Greatest Ways of Getting the Order (or at Least Your Own Way)

Introduction

Rudyard Kipling's famous five friends 'Who, what, when, where and why' is probably the first documentation of the 'open' question. Most business people use open questions to elicit information from customers, markets, colleagues and so on. Everyone is aware that if you ask the right open question you can get people to talk about themselves, what they do and what they like.

But actual progress in business is made with the frequent asking of closed questions – questions that look for one word answers, often 'yes' or 'no'. It is by closing for agreement that you become aware of whether or not you are going to get your own way, what salespeople call 'getting the order'. One of the greatest business ideas, therefore, has to be to hone your skills in asking closing questions and set stretching but achievable objectives every time you communicate with colleagues, customers and suppliers.

'It's so frustrating when you do not tell us what you want us to do or what you want us to agree to' said the Chairman of the Board to a middle manager at the end of a presentation. The manager had requested an opportunity to make a half-hour pitch to his senior colleagues. He had been talking about a new channel of distribution that he was in the process of setting up, and the reason he had asked for the meeting was to help to remove an uncomfortable feeling that some other managers did not think the new idea as brilliant as he did. He felt he needed 'top cover'.

Such scenes are played out in business millions of times a day. It's strange but true that while very few managers nowadays would think of operating without some agreed objectives and measures of performance, they frequently communicate, be it by a letter, a meeting, a telephone call or a presentation, without first of all thinking what they want to get agreement to, i.e. what their objective is in communicating.

Such managers should learn from salespeople, who use closing techniques throughout a sales campaign to make sure that they are on course to their final objective of a sale. It is hard to find the source of the greatest closing techniques as they have been around for ever, or at least since people tried to persuade others to follow their line of thought or action.

We'll start with the one that even the most seasoned salespeople sometimes get wrong. It happens when, in a competitive situation, the prospective customer tells the salesperson that they have a problem with price.

Idea 29 – Trial closing a price objection

A group of professionals in a chartered surveyors firm were discussing what they should say to clients who tell them that they have other quotations which are cheaper than their's. Here is a selection of their replies.

- 'If you pay peanuts you get monkeys.'
- 'But the other firms do not have the experience that we have in this area.'
- 'We'll match their price' (i.e. give away most of the profit).
- 'We have been established for over a hundred years.'
- 'We are the Rolls Royce of the chartered surveying business.'

It is obvious what they were getting at, but none of these responses would be in the objection handling bag of a professional salesperson. Indeed some professional salespeople might describe the professional chartered surveyors' remarks as bullshit.

The worst response of those above is probably the offer to match the competitor's price. Salespeople feel that, say, 10% off the price is not a big deal, because they do not realise what it does to the bottom line. Here's an example of this from the insurance business.

Ruining sales by discounting commissions

The original commission rate is 20%

Premium	£1000
Cost of insurance	£800
Gross margin	£200
Expenses	£50
Net profit	£150

Under pressure the salesperson discounts the premium by 10%

Premium	£900
Cost of insurance	£800
Gross margin	£100
Expenses	£50
Net profit	£50

A 10% reduction in the premium is a 66% reduction in the bottom line

---

No, the correct way to handle a price objection is to use the trial close. It goes like this:

'If we were the same price would you prefer our proposal?'

What is the client to say? Suppose they say 'Well no actually,' seemingly the worst outcome, at least you can now ask 'Why?' and deal with the other objections, real or imagined. Suppose they say 'Well, yes I think we would.' At that point the same question 'Why?' will elicit what the client believes are your advantages as opposed to the general statements above. Often in this last case, the clients are actually trying to persuade themselves that the bit extra is worth it.

Incidentally the other selling technique that is tested by this method of handling price objections is the ability to remain silent. Frequently the 'Would you buy from us if we were the same price as the cheapest?' question leads to a lot of thought from the prospect. Keep your mouth shut and wait for the response.

Frequently the 'Would you buy from us if we were the same price as the cheapest?' question leads to a lot of thought from the prospect. Keep your mouth shut and wait for the response.

Idea 30 – The puppy dog close

This close is based on the activities of a person who sell pets. 'Look' he says to Mum and Dad, 'why don't you take the puppy home for the weekend and see how the kids get on with it. No obligation, if you don't want it I'll come round Monday and take it away.' What with? A small army?

The salesperson knows that by the end of the weekend the kids will be as willing to give up the little dog as they are to give up breathing or having a birthday. This technique is used by many industries in various ways, and is linked to the idea of making sales by inertia. When did you last get an offer to send in a direct debit for a magazine subscription with the promise that no debits would be made until you had received your four free issues? That's a puppy dog close.

They are using it for credit cards nowadays and even IT equipment and software. It works where the product once experimented with becomes highly desirable or where the customer continues with the product because they don't know how to stop it coming, or they can't be bothered. Book clubs would hardly exist without this close.

I have just received the *Wall Street Journal* free for four weeks. In the end I declined to pay for it in future and sent the direct debit confirmation back marked 'Cancelled.' They sent me another one to make sure, with the extraordinary PS

'This is a *risk-free* offer. If you choose not to continue, the four weeks are yours to keep free of charge.' You mean there was a risk they might have asked for their old newspapers back?

Idea 31 – The cup of coffee close

Many decisions in business are taken by a group of people, a committee or a board for example, and many a sale has been lost because the seller is unaware of the cup of coffee close.

The manager has made his pitch, or the salesperson his final presentation to a group of decision-making managers. It is the easiest thing in the world for the chairman to thank the speaker for making the case so well, and say that the managers will give it serious thought and discussion. The meeting ends with no decision because the chairman actually does want to hear everyone's views before a decision is confirmed. If they decide against, they can tell the salesperson by phone or by letter, always easier than face to face.

Pre-empt the situation with the cup of coffee close. If it feels good and the vibrations are positive, offer to leave the group on its own for ten minutes. 'Look it must be difficult for you to make a decision while I am here, I'll go and have a cup of coffee while you have a chat. I'll pop back in a few minutes.' Either they are going to agree to your suggestion, a buying sign, tell you it is not necessary for you to go, another buying sign, or they are going to say that it is not necessary for you to return and that they will get back to you in due course, probably a warning signal.

It's quite fun if they agree to your returning in a few minutes. If when you return everyone looks at you, you have got the order. If only the Chairman is looking at you and some people are having their own quiet discussion you can be sure you have more work to do or that you have lost.

Idea 32 – It's as easy as ABC – Always Be Closing

We do not know who first coined this phrase but it's spot on. Ginger up your communication skills by practising and using good closing and trial closing technique.

Salesman: 'Which of the colours fits best with your kitchen decoration – the grey or the light blue?' This is called an alternative close.

Manager: 'If you had those resources would you take responsibility for achieving that objective?' Trial close.

Mother: 'If you had your own clothing allowance would you keep your room tidy?' Associated project close.

Teenager: 'But everyone's getting them, so if you don't buy me them now there will be none left.' Impending event close.

Idea 33 – Tell them what you are going to ask for

If you have to persuade someone to change their minds or move from a neutral position on a decision to a positive one, it is easy to duck the issue at the beginning of your persuasive activity. Again using the medium of a presentation, let us look at this.

You are trying to get agreement to the board putting two new people into your team over six months to take charge of arranging trade shows. Prior to this the trade shows had somehow happened, but with a lot of last-minute panic and favours being asked of various people within and without the company. These last-minute panics tend to cost a lot of money as the alternative of not being ready for opening day is unacceptable. (How much does an electrician charge per hour when it is 6 o'clock in the evening before the show opens and your stand has, at present, a temporary spotlight?) The professionalism of your exhibits is also, you are convinced, inferior to the other companies at the show.

The board is likely to be sceptical since this is new expenditure with no exceptional new results.

From what has gone before in this section you have prepared your closing question. 'Do I have your agreement to go out to the usual recruitment agency and instruct them to hire two grade 4s straight away?' It's nice and specific with no room for ambiguity or subsequent backsliding.

Now think about your opening. A lot of people would fudge the opening, preferring to launch into horror stories of what has happened in the past, showing the board the list of extra shows that you could put on if you had the resources and so on. This tends to put the board on its guard. Remember, very few managers go to the board with any suggestion that does not require additional resources and it is frustrating when they do not have a clue about how much you are going to ask for.

Remember, very few managers go to the board with any suggestion that does not require additional resources and it is frustrating when they do not have a clue about how much you are going to ask for.

Much better is to signal the closing question right at the beginning of the presentation. It goes something like this:

'You have given me ten minutes so I'll get to the point as quickly as possible. I am going to cover three topics in the ten minutes. First I am going to go over the current situation we face in arranging and setting up exhibition stands, then I am going to ask your permission to hire two extra grade 4 people to carry out that role in the future, and with any time that is left show you our current ideas for the next big show. Is that OK?'

The insertion of the closed question at the end of this statement can be very revealing. It can lead to a huge row. 'No you bloody well cannot have more people, these shows are more trouble than they are worth already' and so on. At least you are arguing about the point you are trying to make. More often you will get a neutral reply such as 'Yes, OK, but if we have any problems with the first bit, we will not be agreeing to the second bit.' Incidentally, if this remark comes from the most senior person in the room it will generally get a laugh, which is always good. Sometimes you will get a more positive response and you will wonder why you are making the presentation at all.

Whatever happens you will have made real progress towards getting a decision and your own way.

Here comes the twist

- Look at a letter you have written or a presentation you have given and see whether the objective was specific and that you clearly asked if you had achieved it.
- Think about your next meeting, what you are trying to persuade people of, and plan the closing question and then the opening.

*F*our *G*reatest *D*oor-to-*D*oor *S*alesmen

Introduction

Door-to-door selling has rather a bad name nowadays. Most people I mention it to respond with 'double glazing' and 'knife sharpening'. But many other products have become successful through this medium, and some large companies built. You can buy cosmetics (*Idea 36*) or cleaning products (*Idea 35*), but I start with what was a genuine win–win for door-to-door sales technique, good for the company and good for the householder.

Idea 34 – Security from cradle to grave (Prudential)

In 1948 The Prudential Mutual Assurance, Investment and Loan Association was formed to serve the needs of the British professional classes. Their loan and life products were offered only to the affluent. Companies at the time were unwilling to take on the risks involved in insuring the working classes.

It was a deputation of factory workers combined with a recommendation from Parliament that persuaded the company to issue life policies for small sums. The fear of the poor, that they would not have a proper funeral, led to life policies for small sums, with weekly or monthly payments to cover, in the first place, funeral costs.

The industrial department opened in 1854 and appointed agents to sell 'penny policies' to Victorian workers. Industrial insurance quickly became the most important part of the company's business.

A leading light in all of this was Henry Harben, the secretary of the company. He put down values of simple product design, effective distribution and efficient service. The door-to-door salespeople were central to all of these values.

Growth was steady and by time the Industrial Division was 25 years old, it was necessary for new headquarters to be found. In 1879 the building, which is still its HQ, was opened in Holborn Bars. The Pru was also engaged in the pioneering work of the day, to introduce women into the work force. The new building included facilities for women clerks.

The company's publicity material records that 'By the end of the century, Prudential was well-established as the leading insurer in Britain regarded as a national institution more than a commercial company. Across the country, one person in three held a Prudential policy.'

In the first half of the twentieth century the Prudential co-operated with the government in collecting contributions to the state sickness and unemployment scheme. The branding of the Prudential as more than a commercial company continued with the ending of gender segregation in offices. They also took on women and retired men to replace those called up for World War I and did not charge extra premiums to enlisted men. This time period also saw the expansion of the company into overseas markets, with a network of agencies across Europe and the British Empire.

After World War II the Prudential started to use their agent organisation as part of their advertising, and a real agent, Fred Sawyer from Kent, became well known all over the world as the Man from the Pru.

From the 1970s most expansion came from the acquisition of other companies. The Prudential is now a market leader in most areas of personal finance. There are no door-to-door Men from the Pru now; they have been replaced by higher-tech ways of doing business.

Prudential reported total sales of £4.4 billion in the first nine months of 2002, 12 per cent up on the same period the previous year. It owns a fund manager and a bank. Along with other life companies that it owns it is still a massive player in the global insurance sector. But the business was built on door-to-door collection agents guaranteeing that poorer people could have a decent funeral.

> **Ask yourself**
>
> • When did you last check that you had the right amount of life insurance? By the time they get to middle age, a lot of people when they add it all up find that they have too much life insurance and not enough long term or pension savings.

Idea 35 – 'We'll over the Border and gi'e them a brush' – James Hogg (Kleeneze)

It is a startling tribute to their salespeople, that, as children, my sister and I looked forward to the arrival of the man with the caseful of brushes, clothes and polishes – the Kleeneze man. We liked the little free samples of polish he gave kids, which we used for polishing dolls' shoes and Hornby trains, respectively.

The story of Kleeneze starts with a young man emigrating with his family to the USA. There he discovered the Fuller Brush Company, who sold door to door high quality brushes using twisted-in-wire methodology. So impressed was he that he came back to the UK and in Bristol started the Kleeneze company. The man's name was Harry Crook, as unlikely a name for anyone in the selling game as any you could think of. In fact if you can sell door to door with the name Crook on your business card, you must be able, as they say, to sell pork chops to a rabbi.

Kleeneze claims to be the first company in Britain selling door to door, and the first to introduce network marketing (see *Amway Idea 9*).

The company, which operates in the UK and the Republic of Ireland, has traded profitably every year since 1923. There are 12,000 distributors, a number that is still said to be growing, who deliver catalogues and deliver door to door. They also recruit new distributors to take advantage of a sales-based commission scheme. Sales in 1998 were £39 million with profits of over £3 million.

The case of samples has gone, replaced by a catalogue containing over 600 items. The range has increased as well. It still has the *Homecare* section with cleaning materials and tools. To this it has added *Home ideas*, *Personal care*, *What's cooking* and *Garden & workshop*. The catalogue is attractive and comprehensive, but I wonder if children rush indoors to tell their mothers that the Kleeneze catalogue is coming.

Idea 36 – Ding doing well (Avon)

The first 'Avon Lady,' Mrs. P.F.E. Albee of Winchester, NH, pioneered the company's now-famous direct-selling method. By so doing Avon provided one of the first opportunities for American women to be financially independent at a time when their place was traditionally at home. Indeed, women have sold Avon since 1886, that is 34 years before they won the right to vote!

Avon Products, Inc., founded in 1886, is the world's largest direct seller of beauty and related products. With $4.8 billion in annual revenues, the company ranks 293rd on the Fortune 500 list of America's largest companies. It markets to women in 131 countries through nearly 2.3 million independent sales representatives.

'Avon' is among the world's largest selling brands of cosmetics, fragrances and toiletries, including such recognisable brands as *Anew, Avon Skin Care, Skin-So-Soft, Avon Color, Far Away, Rare Gold, Josie, Natori,* and *Millennia*. In addition, the company is one of the world's largest manufacturers of fashion jewellery. It also markets an extensive line of apparel, gifts, decorative, collectible, and family entertainment products. Avon's vision is: to be the company that best understands and satisfies the product, service and self-fulfilment needs of women – globally. This vision influences the company's research, product development, marketing and management practices.

This emphasis on women, as well as the door-to-door aspect of their selling, makes it a highly innovative company. The statistics tell the tale.

Avon has more women in management positions (86%) than any other Fortune 500 company. Seventeen of Avon's 54 officers (32%) are women and four women sit on Avon's board of directors. Avon's Women of Enterprise Awards program, created in 1987 in conjunction with the US Small Business Administration, annually recognises five women entrepreneurs for extraordinary business success.

Since October 1993, the Avon Breast Cancer Awareness Crusade has raised $25 million to support breast-cancer education and access to early detection services. The company in 1993 established the Avon World-wide Fund for Women's Health to raise money for health-related problems of concern to women globally.

The company has a trail of awards for employment practices including six entries in the 100 Best Companies for Working Mothers. It is also recognised by its policies and practices in encouraging ethnic minorities such as Hispanic and black people.

Approximately 50% of American women have purchased from Avon in the last year; 90% have done so in their lifetime.

Avon's 100% money-back guarantee was instituted 111 years ago – the day the company was founded – and Avon sees itself as the supplier of prestige-quality beauty products at affordable prices.

Certainly their reach to consumers through direct selling is very impressive. Each year, Avon prints over 600 million sales brochures in more than 12 languages. In the US alone, the brochure is distributed to 14 million women every two weeks. Nearly half the women in the US, 48 million, rely on Avon and its beauty products. To reach today's women, 30% of Avon representatives sell in offices, factories, hospitals, schools – wherever women work. Approximately 50% of American women have purchased from Avon in the last year; 90% have done so in their lifetime.

Idea 37 – Forecasting a sale

In the 1950s there was a Indian guru who was trying to be a mystic; he had a small following, but at the same time he had to earn a living. This he did by selling Indian products – shawls, tablecloths and other decorative fabrics – door to door. Wittingly or unwittingly, he developed a pretty eccentric impending event close (see *greatest ways of getting the order Idea 33*). Once the housewife had looked at the offerings and was plainly about to decline, the fakir moved to his other persona and offered to tell her fortune.

Studying her hand intently, he pursed his lips and gave the sort of Delphic prophecies you would expect from such an exercise. He was good at it and normally got the attention of the prospect with a few good 'hits' on things that were actually true. At the end of the consultation, he would suddenly notice another line on the hand and exclaim, 'Oh, I see that you and I will never meet again!' 'Really?' said the customer. 'Yes,' said the guru, 'So this is your only opportunity to buy these rugs, shawls and tablecloths.'

Six Greatest Financial Necessities of Business Life

Introduction

Good business comes from innovation, risk and customer satisfaction. But we do need a simple measure to keep control. Whilst it is possible to be a sales manager with a less than rudimentary knowledge of, say, production, it is not possible to be an anything manager without a good passing knowledge of finance. This section outlines those basic great ideas that allow finance to be an enabler and encourager of business.

The concept of money and interest (*Idea 39*) leads through limited companies (*Idea 40*) and double-entry book-keeping (*Idea 41*) to the all-important financial ratios that determine the health of a company (*Idea 42*). Finally, we come to the best way of estimating the financial future of projects and proposals (*Idea 43*). But we start with a short nightmare.

Idea 38 – *Even* Turing Idea 44 *needed Arabic numerals*

If Arabic numbers had not been developed, the chances are we would still be counting in Roman numerals. Have a go at these simple sums without resorting to Arabic numerals:

1   MDCXXI + LCCIV
2   DIV – CCCVII
3   CCCVI × XI

The answers are given in Appendix 1.

Idea 39 – How the total money supply is greater than the total amount of money

'Money is the root of all evil, and yet it is such a useful root that we cannot get on without it any more than we can without potatoes.'

Louisa Alcott Brown (1832–88)

I once was the sales manager for a computer company, and managed to make a sale to a Nigerian businessman. The sale was progressing rather smoothly, when I discovered that he had answered my questions about having the resources to buy the machine very widely. He had the resources, but not the money. I was eventually paid, through an agent, with a shipload of cement. My problem was to get the cement off my asset list before the month-end accounts were calculated and the finance department became aware of what I had done. This one fling with barter taught me not to do it again. Even babysitting credits went wrong when we got involved. Business depends on money, but it is a very difficult concept to understand.

The paradox in the title is at the root of the whole of commerce. Before coming to it let us look at the economic purposes of money. In standard economic theory money is said to have four distinct but interrelated functions:

1   To serve as a medium of exchange universally accepted in exchange for goods or services.
2   To act as a measure of value, a common yardstick which makes the operation of the price system possible and provides the basis for keeping records.
3   To serve as a standard of deferred payments, the unit in which loans are made and future transactions fixed. Without money there could be no commonly accepted basis for borrowing and lending and the concept of credit could not play its huge role in the organisation and encouragement of business.

4   To provide a store of wealth, a convenient form in which to hold any income not needed for immediate use. It is the only truly liquid asset, the only one that can be readily converted into other goods.

The complexity of money increased enormously with the abandonment by most countries of the gold standard. Up until the 1930s the issuers of banknotes promised to exchange them for a given amount of gold or silver. The depressions of the 1920s changed all that, and paper money is now issued on the general creditworthiness of the country of issue.

To most individuals money consists of coins, banknotes and the readily usable deposits held in banks and other financial institutions. To the economy, however, the total money supply is many times as large as the sum total of individual money holdings defined in this way. This is because a very large proportion of the deposits placed with financial institutions is loaned out, thus multiplying the overall money supply several times over.

Without this device and the concept of interest, the economies of developed and developing countries could not happen at the present pace. It should continue to work, at least until we all decide that we want our money back at the same time.

Idea 40 – Raising cash with limited liability

In the introduction we said that one of the biggest necessities of any great idea was to sell it. To sell a product, great idea or not, you need first to produce it. To produce it you need money up front. If you have money and no great ideas, you need to get someone else to use your cash and earn a return. The joint stock company is the vehicle that brings these two things together.

The Joint Stock Companies Act, as amended in 1855, permitted such companies to limit the liability of their members, shareholders, to the nominal value of their shares. In effect, by applying for a £1 share, a shareholder agreed to subscribe

£1 and was not liable for any further contribution in the event of the company's insolvency.

Leading from the joint stock company is the need for a set of rules that managers have to obey in order to give a fair picture of the financial health of the enterprise. This is the audit.

The repercussions of the simple idea of shareholder investment are legion. Ideas that would never have got started became possible and the current system of equities was born.

Takeovers became possible. Takeovers are a pretty good business idea if you are one of the army of professional accountants, bankers and lawyers who charge fat fees for making them happen, sometimes, some would say, at the expense of shareholders and workers. Takeovers also give the directors of the larger entity more power and bigger salaries.

Convertible loan stock is a system whereby the shareholder takes a reduced risk for the certainty of return in the early stages of an investment. Indeed it is possible to describe the attributes of shares in any way that suits the board and the shareholders. Without these devices, for example, *Eurotunnel Idea 22* would have long since sunk.

On the other hand

The limited company enables individuals to walk away from the mess they have created under its protection, and then do it all over again somewhere else.

The company audit enables shareholders to sleep at night while risking bankruptcy. It is very similar to the insurance policy that permits the householder to sleep at night while their house is burgled. When they wake up to a calamity they discover, because of the small print, that they actually have no redress at all

Idea 41 – Keeping score positively

The *South Sea Bubble Idea 79* stayed in the mind of business people for many years, and the concept of stewardship followed the invention of the joint stock company to allay the fears of would-be investors. Stewardship involves the orderly recording of business transactions and the presentation of summary reports. This is pejoratively known as bean counting, but can be of great value to the people running the business.

The main principles of what became double-entry book-keeping emerged in Italy at the time of the renaissance. They were based on a treatise by Luca Paciolito and reflected the growing complexity of business life. The development of book-keeping and accountancy reflects the history of commerce.

It has three main purposes:

1   as a check against fraud and error
2   to assist managers with the information they need to make decisions
3   as the basis for the accounting practices that give rise to the audit.

Whilst book-keeping can become highly complex, basically there are two types of books used in the book-keeping process: journals and ledgers. A journal contains the daily transactions (sales, purchases and so on) and the ledger keeps the record of individual accounts.

From that basis each month the income statement presents the changes that have occurred over the period in question, while the balance sheet shows the financial state of a company at a point in time in terms of assets, liabilities and the ownership equity.

Nowadays accountants can and do play a most constructive role in the management of businesses. At least the enlightened ones do; the others just keep the score.

Nowadays accountants can and do play a most constructive role in the management of businesses. At least the enlightened ones do; the others just keep the score.

Idea 42 – How well are we doing?

An essential driver of business is its performance against the most common ratios used by boards of directors and shareholders. Here are eight ratios that are frequently used.

Return on capital employed

This is often considered to be the main indicator of the profitability of a business. After all, the basis of enterprise is to take money in the form of share capital and loan capital and use it to earn profits. This RoCE percentage is a good guide to the performance of managers in producing sufficient return. A sudden alteration for better or worse will give rise to further investigation to see what has changed.

Profit margin

This shows the profits made on each pound of sales. As businesses grow their managers are concerned over time to maintain a good 'bottom line profit margin'. It is quite reasonable that peaks and troughs will occur. For example, where a company has been involved in a major expansion, it may take some time, measured in years, to get back to its original profit margin and then exceed it.

Return on assets

This ratio is more important in some industries than others. Basically the clue is the amount of investment in fixed assets required to create a going concern. In a firm of consultants, for example, where there are few fixed assets since arguably the main assets are the people acting as consultants, this ratio will have little relevance. In the case of a telephone company with the hugely expensive asset of the network, this ratio is crucial.

Return on shareholders' funds

This ratio measures management's ability to use the share capital in the business efficiently and produce good returns. There is a tendency to use this measure as a final measure of profitability. In some ways it is a more logical measure of return than RoCE, since the latter ratio is lowered by the inclusion of loan capital in capital employed. Some would argue that because the interest on loan capital has already been deducted from net profit before tax, then the providers of the loan capital have already had their return and should be excluded from the capital employed. That is the case with this ratio.

Economic value added (EVA)

This is also known as economic profit, and is defined as the difference between net profit after tax and the cost of the capital employed in the business. This is said to be an important indicator of managers' real created value. It certainly has a benefit internally as managers who are targeted on EVA are forced to realise constantly that all capital has a cost.

Market value added (MVA)

Very much linked to EVA, market value added takes the market capitalisation of a business and subtracts the total of its capital employed. Assuming this is positive, MVA is said to put a value on the 'stock market wealth created'.

In summary, EVA tries to show the return to shareholders on an annual basis, while MVA attempts to show the total return.

Added value

The difference between the market value of a company's outputs and the cost of its inputs. An improving trend here should augur a successful performance. The main problem is to get the necessary data to make the calculation from published material.

Total shareholder return

This measures the return to shareholders from dividend income and capital gains in the value of the shares. It can take time into account by discounting income and gains made to present value, and is a very useful tool of comparison between one share and another.

Idea 43 – Never mind the profit, feel the cashflow

There once was a computer salesman, we'll call him George, trying to sell his wares to a company that sold and fitted tyres and exhausts for all models of car. He got on well with the managing director and the sales director. With his help they were starting to see the business benefits of using a computer to take over from a complicated card system, which was how they controlled the stock. This was a long time ago.

Our salesman felt reasonably confident that the order was his, until he was mugged by the finance director, not with a physical blunt instrument but rather with the esoteric blunt instrument of a discounted cashflow.

'In this company' announced the finance man, 'we test all our capital investment projects against a hurdle rate of return, currently set at 21%.' The salesman understood neither the term hurdle rate of return nor how you arrived at the 21%.

The sales director explained the system using words, which first amazed George and then started to unfold some of the mysteries of how companies make decisions. 'The managing director and I make all the major decisions in this company,' he started, 'and our gut feel has a reasonably impressive track record. However, with the onset of shareholder capital and a new finance director we had to put in place some of the business processes that executives, particularly finance executives, find so necessary. One of the first was the system for financially evaluating purchases, particularly capital expenditure.

'This consists of a cost–benefit analysis and some risk analysis to assess the downside of things going wrong. Finally it lands on the desk of financial controllers, who put the numbers from the cost–benefit analysis into a discounted cashflow. It is a useful, though not vital, test of all projects. It allows us to compare one strategy with another, or, for example, the relative financial merit of buying a computer against the totally different proposal to open more depots. It is important, and if you are going to work with us you had better learn how it works. Having said that, if projects look good to the MD and me, they usually go ahead.'

George went through the learning process.

Why do we need discounted cashflow?

Once managers have done some sort of cost–benefit analysis on how they would like the company's resources to be spent, their bosses have the job of deciding which ones to accept and which to reject. How do they compare one project with another?

Consider the following projects (both of five years duration)

	Project 1	Project 2
Initial investment	£10,000	£10,000
Expected annual earnings		
(before depreciation)		
Year 1	2,000	5,000
Year 2	3,000	6,000
Year 3	5,000	7,000
Year 4	7,000	4,000
Year 5	8,000	3,000
Total	25,000	25,000
Net earnings over 5 years	15,000	15,000

Which would you choose?

Both of these projects give the same total profit over five years but I imagine that, all other things being equal, most people would prefer to undertake project 2 since the returns arise earlier.

That problem was easy to solve, but what if the return on project 2 in year five was only £2,000? Would the reduced total profit on project 2 now make it less desirable than project 1 or is the advantage of early payback great enough to overcome the disadvantage of reduced profit?

The mechanics of DCF

To arrive at a method of dealing with this, consider the following:

You have inherited £10,000 from Aunt Mary. Unfortunately, she had heard that you are liable to spend money fairly freely, so her will says that you cannot receive the cash until your 30th birthday. You are 27 today (happy birthday!)

Aunt Mary was actually fairly well informed. You are desperate to get this money before the 3.30 at Aintree and you have found a friendly banker who will advance you part of the money.

The interest rate is 10% per annum and she is prepared to advance you an amount £A such that with interest you will owe her exactly £10,000 in three years time. How much can you get? See if you can work it out before you turn the page to the solution.

If someone borrows £100 now, they will owe interest of £10 by the end of one year so the total outstanding will be £110.

During the second year, interest will be charged on the total amount outstanding of £110 i.e. interest of £11. The total outstanding would be £121.

During the third year, interest will be charged on the total amount outstanding of £121 i.e. interest of £12.10. The total outstanding would then be £133.10.

We can see therefore that for every £100 borrowed, £133.10 must be repaid.

Therefore, solving the equation:

$$£A \times 1.331 = £10,000$$

will tell us how much can be borrowed now, i.e. about £7,510.

This technique can of course be generalised to deal with any rate of interest and any time period.

We can now develop a method to compare two projects. Cashflows due in the future may be converted to equally desirable cashflows due today using the above method. This technique is known as discounting and the equivalent cashflow due today is known as a present value. This is shown in the following example.

Timing of cashflow	Amount of cashflow	Discount factor at 10%*	Present value
Immediate	(10,000)	1	(10,000)
After 1 year	3,000	0.909	2,727
After 2 years	4,000	0.826	3,304
After 3 years	5,000	0.751	3,755
After 4 years	3,000	0.683	2,049
Net present value	£1,835		

*Discount factors may be found from tables or by using the formula
$1/(1 + i)^n$
where i = discount rate, n = number of years.

In particular, consider the discount factor used above for year three, i.e. 0.751. When deciding how much we could borrow from the bank in respect of Aunt Mary's bequest we divided £10,000 by 1.331. An exactly equivalent calculation is performed by multiplying £10,000 by 0.751 – the discount factor for three years at 10%.

The final result takes into account all cashflows and is known as the net present value of the project.

If compelled to choose between two projects, we will select the one with the higher net present value. If we have a large number of projects that can all be undertaken, then we should invest in every project that has a positive net present value.

In effect the discounting factor brings the value of each number into today's money, present value, thus ensuring that you are comparing pounds now with pounds to be earned or spent in the future.

What can you use DCF for?

The discounted cashflow and net present value earns its place in the 100 greatest business ideas by its simple ability to put the logical case behind dilemmas or decisions. Other methods, such as payback or average rate of return, all run dangers that a decision that looks good using that method of appraisal will turn out to be a disaster.

As well as in a business environment, DCF has a role in any individual's financial plan. Here are some ways that you can use it in your personal financial life.

The discounted cashflow and net present value earns its place in the 100 greatest business ideas by its simple ability to put the logical case behind dilemmas or decisions.

- You can solve the problem of rent or buy. While the UK Government gave tax relief on mortgage repayments it tended to be a relatively straightforward decision to buy the home you live in rather than rent it. This has become less certain as the tax benefit has gone and it is theoretically worth making a comparison to check that financially it remains the thing to do.

- Using a similar cashflow you could examine a project to invest in buying a property for you to rent out to tenants.
- How do you compare the performance of equity shares in a personal portfolio? If you simply look at capital growth you will be biased towards companies that have enjoyed growth irrespective of whether they have also produced dividend return. You will also find it difficult to make comparisons if you have bought shares at different times or added to the holding of one share during the period you are trying to compare. The answer is the DCF technique. An example of holding BP shares over a period of time is shown in Appendix 2.

Imagine if *unit trust managers Idea 25* had to publish their real results in such terms. Might not the consumer get a very different opinion?

Ask yourself

- Do you really understand discounted cashflows? If not do some more work on it.
- Somewhere in your working environment someone will be using investment appraisal techniques that affect you. It might be the finance department in your own company, or your suppliers, or your customers. It might even be the people who are planning your pension, i.e. the people who are responsible for how poor you are going to be in your late old age. Find out how they do it.

So how, after all this learning, did George fare? He sat down with the sales director and worked out the likely benefits of the new stock control system. The main benefit of course was rather intangible, i.e. difficult to put a number to. It related to the fact that if the system were better there would be fewer stock outs and therefore they would sell more tyres and exhausts. After some bargaining the sales director agreed that he would stand by a claim of 5% more sales. And so on. He built a case for the benefits.

With the IT manager, George built a picture of the costs over a five-year period, found that the project was profitable, but needed help to see if this was confirmed by the cashflow. With some trepidation George went to see the finance director, who took him through the calculation. Using the discount factor of 21%, the company norm, the project ended up with a negative net present value. George was devastated.

He returned to the sales director crestfallen to report that all their work had ended up torpedoed by the finance people. The sales director looked at the cashflow and suggested that George should see if the case worked if he, the sales director, agreed that a 10% sales increase was a more likely outcome. It did and George got the order and a lot wiser.

*E*ight *G*reatest *C*omputer *I*nnovations
*that A*ctually *M*ake *L*ife *E*asier

Introduction

As an enabler of great business ideas, probably nothing has approached the digital computer. It permeates the lives of everyone in the western world and has in a remarkably short time created business opportunities that could only have been a dream without it. How then do we choose the greatest ideas in this realm? We have chosen a timeline of developments that slowly but surely made computers useful and fun.

As an enabler of great business ideas, probably nothing has approached the digital computer.

It was at the outset a mathematical tool, and it is worth looking at what that means using the example of *iteration Idea 45* and *critical path analysis Idea 46*. After that there is the *database Idea 47* technologies, which enabled much of the information that gives birth to other great ideas, as did *spreadsheets Idea 48*.

When the first personal computers came out their advertisements vied for new ways to express the term 'user friendly.' But whatever the ads may have said, a reviewer who tried to take a PC out of its box, switch it on and use it was probably nearer the truth when he described them as 'as user friendly as a cornered rat'. The *graphical user interface Idea 49* changed that and earns its place in the 100 greatest, as does *Windows Idea 50*.

We then switch to an idea that gets a mixed reception but is almost certainly a force for consumer satisfaction in the long term – the *call centre Idea 51*.

But we start at the beginning with the mathematician who first developed the basic mathematical idea of a mechanical process for reliable and consistent calculation.

Idea 44 – Turing's table of behaviour

'Bernard of Chartres used to say that we are like dwarfs on the shoulders of giants, so that we can see more than they, and things at greater distance, not by virtue of any sharpness of sight on our part, or any physical distinction but because we are carried high and raised up by their giant size.'

John of Salisbury, 1159

Alan Turing, who is generally credited with the invention of the basics behind the digital computer, can justly claim to be one of the giants on whose shoulders stand many others. He developed his concept of a table of behaviour in the mid-1930s as his contribution to a question posed by the mathematician David Hilbert.

The question was 'Is mathematics decidable?' Was there a definite method which, when applied, in principle, to any assertion, could be guaranteed to give a correct decision as to whether the assertion was true or false. The answer that Turing came up with was 'Yes, by a mechanical process.'

He searched for an 'automatic machine' that would require no human intervention. It must be capable of reading a mathematical assertion and eventually writing a decision as to whether the assertion could be proven or not.

This led to the table of behaviour. Turing saw it as a tape marked off into squares. The tape was definite, but of unlimited length. The tape passes by what Turing called a scanner at a fixed point, which is capable of reading whether each square contains a 1 or is blank. The machine is capable also of writing 1 into a blank square and returning a square containing 1 to blank by erasing it.

A limited number of 'configurations' is then required for the machine to be able to do calculations. You can think of configurations by thinking of a typewriter with two configurations: upper and lower case.

It requires only four configurations, to move the tape right or left, write 1 or erase 1, to carry out additions.

So, from that teasingly simple basis the rest is history.

Turing went on to work as the mathematical genius of Bletchley Park, where he did more than anyone to make possible the breaking of the Enigma codes and give the allies certain information of the strategy and tactics of the axis powers in World War II.

A colleague at Bletchley Park, Donald Michie, a classics scholar from Balliol College, Oxford, and subsequently an expert on computers and the Professor of machine intelligence at Edinburgh University, spoke thus of Turing.

'Alan Turing is one of the figures of the century. His consequences are everywhere and nobody knows now where it is going to take us. The world of computing and now the world of the Internet stems from Alan Turing's fundamental ideas. There were other great men in Bletchley Park, but in the long long wall of history I think Turing's name will probably be the number one in terms of consequences for mankind.'

Idea 45 – Getting the answer through trial and error

A combination of a human feel for the solution to a problem, usually mathematical, and the power of a computer has enabled many new insights into equations. The process is called iteration. Taking as an example the formula to find the square root of a number. The iterative process is

$$X_n = \frac{X_{n-1}^2 + a}{2X_{n-1}}$$

where a is the number whose square root is required, we will gradually get to a better and better approximation to the answer. Suppose we wanted to use iteration to find the square root of 2. If we start with

$$X_1 = 1$$

we get:

$$X_2 = 1.5$$
$$X_3 = 1.417$$
$$X_4 = 1.414$$

so that with only three steps we have reached a very good approximation. It would have taken many more iterations if our original guess had been much wider of the mark. If, for example, we had started with $X_1 = 50$ it would have taken nine iterations to get to the same point. The iterative process is continued until any desired accuracy, tested for by the computer, is reached.

This is a very simple example. There are many extremely useful and sometimes sophisticated iterative processes for solving various types of equation. Iteration is also used in routines that are closer to business needs, such as sorting tables of data. It is unlikely that all equations can be solved by iterative methods, but the computer has certainly extended vastly the number that can be tackled in this way.

But it comes down in the end to a combination of man and machine. The better the guess, from a better feel for the problem, the fewer steps it takes.

Idea 46 – When it's critical to be on time and within budget

There are many instances where computer power has enabled a mathematical process to be used where, with only brain and pencil power, the number of calculations required to do something useful make it quite impossible. Perhaps a good example of this came early in the development of computers when they were programmed to work out critical paths for projects.

To carry out critical path analysis, each separate event and activity of a project is assembled into a network. The resources required and the time to complete is then appended. If there is doubt about timescale or resources an optimistic, pessimistic and most likely estimate is used. The network on its own is a useful tool since it points out to the designer or project manager the inter-relationships involved in the project.

Then the computer comes into its own. The critical path of vital core activities is determined by considering each event in turn and calculating the earliest possible time at which the event can occur. The characteristic of events and activities on a critical path is that, if any of the time estimates is not met, the completion date of the project is affected. The other activities are ones with 'float' – that is, an amount of spare time for completion.

When a project includes thousands of activities and interaction with other project networks, it is impossible to conceive of doing the relevant calculations without a computer. Managers look for the following attributes in critical path programmes. It must:

1   handle events and activities and their changing values
2   interrelate networks of different levels
3   accept progress data and produce progress reports
4   determine the critical path through a network.

Ask yourself

Would critical path analysis help to make sure your projects are under better control?

Idea 47 – Connecting up the pieces

If you look in some supermarkets between the hours of 5 and 7 in the evening, you may be surprised to find that there are a number of brands of four packs of beer on shelves beside the disposable nappies. The reason for this is the discovery, made possible by relational databases, that a large number of husbands and partners get a phone call towards the end of the working day requesting that they pick up a packet of disposable nappies on their way home. So the supermarket manager wheels out the four packs and tempts the father into impulse buying a beer to go with the evening television.

This is possible for the supermarket to work out because of the high degree of data integration available to it. There are at least three systems involved in this piece of analysis – the stock control system, the checkout system and the loyalty card system. This strategy is part of the movement towards what the marketing people call 'the market of a single person', where the supplier has access to such a large amount of accessible data that it is able to target a market of one person with the attributes the supplier believes fit the product it is trying to sell.

The technology involved in this has developed over many years. Indeed, some computer salespeople claimed some 25 years ago that what we have now was available then. The underlying technology on which such specific marketing depends is the database and database management systems.

A woman moved to London from Edinburgh. She lived in West Hampstead and worked in the city. Everyday she commuted to work by tube, from Finchley Road to High Holborn. The tube was her only method of transportation for the first few months of her stay in the new location.

After three months if you had asked her how to get to High Holborn from Finchley Road, she could confidently have told you to go past Swiss Cottage to Regents Park. From there make your way to Baker Street and Oxford Circus. She could have directed you all the way by the place names of tube stations, but asked in which direction to walk to start the process of getting to Swiss Cottage she might not have known. That is what computer life was like before databases.

The computer world before databases relied on traditional file processing. Applications systems reflected the previous manual environment. For example, the engineering department of a local authority held a record of all the street furniture, lampposts, benches and so on, in its area. To put these items on to a computer gave the engineers a number of benefits. They could schedule maintenance and repair schedules much more efficiently to make best use of resources and save management time spent on that sort of activity. But the street furniture system had no connection with, for example, the street opening (holes in the road) system.

As more and more systems were computerised, people began to see the need to create reports based on data held in more than one application file. This gave birth to the idea of a central database system.

In a central database system there are still the separate applications systems such as accounts, stock and payroll, but the data for each is held centrally and the individual systems dip into the database in order to process transactions. This leads, at least in theory, to compatibility within systems, less duplication of data since each item is held only once, and thus to more integrity of the data held.

On the other hand

This centralised data concept did not need computers for its implementation, and could lead to two major problems.

1 A growing complexity of the holding of data with its attendant dangers of introducing another set of individuals to look after the central data as well as the application systems.
2 An increase in vulnerability. If all the data is in one place it is more vulnerable to computer malfunction and corruption whether accidental or deliberate.

The computer handles these problems by employing Database Management Systems. This software sits between the database and the systems, and with the use of other powerful tools, such as structured query language, reports can be generated for one-off queries that require investigation of the inter-relationships that might exist between the data sets contained in various databases.

Databases, management systems and structured query language are the road map that connects up the individual tube stations. They offer revolutionary ways of identifying markets. 'Need a nappy, sir? have a beer.'

Ask yourself

Are you aiming your products at the so-called 'market of one'? Are you using collected data, yours and other people's, to home in on the right people with the right products and services?

Idea 48 – Models maketh managers

Try to imagine a world without spreadsheets. You have the task to suggest to the board whether or not a new product project is a viable concept. Either the financial section of the recommendation is going to be pretty weak, with a very limited number of possible outcomes, or you are going to have to do an awful lot of calculations and recalculations. The word 'awful' is used here in its real sense. The alternative is to become dependent on the finance department who will answer financial questions with their function principally in mind. This would be like the spending department ministers in a government being dependent on the treasury to evaluate the financial results of their spending plans.

In the 1970s managers wanted to ask the 'what if' question to test out risk and results in various combinations of eventualities. They knew that a new product broke even in two years if the sales came in on plan, but they did not know, on the down side, at what point the lack of sales would start to threaten the cashflow of the company or the department involved. They did not know, on the upside, when higher than expected sales would push the production people into further invest-ment. But mainly they found it difficult to have a comfortable level of information to compare one investment project with another when the type of investment was very different. They need to be able to ask an infinite number of 'what if' questions.

Various pieces of applications software were written and experimented with, but it was not until the launch of the first spreadsheet system Visicalc in the late 1970s that managers received the ability to create the models they wanted, and to break free from their reliance on the finance department to measure, probably to five decimal places, the financial outcome of the inspired guesses managers make when estimating the future. Computers opened up a totally new planning environment.

The move from dependency on the finance department is rendered useless, of course, if it leads to a new dependency on the computer department.

The move from dependency on the finance department is rendered useless, of course, if it leads to a new dependency on the computer de-partment. Out of the prying department into the technical mire, you might say. Here also spreadsheets offered, and continue to offer, a simple to use mechanism that allows functional managers to create their own models to meet exactly the problem they are trying to solve. Spreadsheets are the antithesis of the general-purpose computer system that solves part of eve-ryone's problem but fails everybody in some way.

The use of the words 'simple' and 'computers' in combination always needs careful examination, remember the cornered rat, but the spreadsheet genuinely can be simple to use. It can then be stretched in a thousand ways to offer complex solutions to complex problems. People who keep learning about them and using them find that they are using not just an upmarket calculating machine capable of producing models, but a powerful programming language of immensely wide value. In fact, even seasoned spreadsheet modellers after some years are still aware that they are only using a fraction of the power of the tool.

It may be slightly esoteric to make a direct link of the work of Turing with the modern day spreadsheet, but the argument has some merit. Essentially spreadsheets allow the user to mix data and logic in a way that reflects how most managers think and plan their businesses. Creative thought and intuition can be quickly tried out at an overall level, formalised and developed according to the answers found to a series of 'what if' questions.

This flexibility makes spreadsheet modelling ideal for managers to analyse a specific situation in a specific way. You can start where you like, for example from sales or fixed costs. You can check that some variables in the middle of the model stay within precisely or loosely defined parameters. You see the result of any formula as you enter it. This makes it likely that you will detect errors early. It also means that you can pause after each step to recognise what you have learnt before moving on.

Opinions vary as to whether spreadsheets are efficient if you take them out of this personal environment and build models intended to be run corporate wide. Intuitively I doubt it.

Experienced modellers volunteer the following tips to help newcomers wield the power of the spreadsheet.

1   Build it step by step. Make sure one month is doing exactly what you want before copying it eleven times.
2   Build the assumptions table outside the model. This means that the top of the spreadsheet has the assumptions that you are going to test, and further down is the actual model.
3   Check each formula as you enter it. Since the assumptions are separate from the model it is easy to enter new assumptions and check their impact on the formula before moving on.
4   Check the overall model by seeing that it behaves as you would expect when you give it new, or even extreme, variables.

5   When, for example, you are happy with the one-month model and you create the next month, error can easily creep in. Try the new month with the same parameters as the original and see that it comes up with the same results.

6   Prepare the model using real prices and costs in the first place. Add in inflation and currency variations at a later stage.

The financial services and insurance industries make much use of laptop computers to aid their salesforce to bring another customer into their net. Spreadsheets enable everybody to do this for whatever product they sell.

In summary, managers have the opportunity to become their own masters if they learn how to bring this most powerful tool into their armoury.

On the other hand

1   Try not to fall into the trap of thinking that the financial criteria are the only ones you need to model. It is still the function of managers to check that other theories, such as life cycles, are taken into account in the planning process.

2   If the situation has changed, start a fresh model or you run the danger of adapting the situation to the model instead of the other way round.

3   Don't let an affair with spreadsheets make you forget other tools for decision making such as plan, execute, reflect and learn.

Idea 49 – Douglas Engelbart: 'the mother of all demos'

This was the phrase one of Engelbart's colleagues used to describe the groundbreaking performance given in a demonstration in 1968. Engelbart had been working for some time on the human–computer interface.

He was a member of the team at the Stanford Research Institute in the late 1950s and early 1960s. Engelbart was a visionary who started from a theoretical framework for the 'co-evolution of human skills knowledge and organisations.' At the heart of his vision was the computer, acting as an extension of human communication capabilities and resource for the 'augmentation of human intellect'.

In other words he worked on getting the computer out of the hands of the technicians and into the working hands of the user. So what did the demonstration contain? Remember that it was 1968 and the computer had had no visibility up until then outside the air-conditioned computer room.

The demonstration, which lasted for 90 minutes, was for most people their first glimpse of a networked computer system. This enabled a series of other firsts. It had the debut of the computer mouse, two-dimensional display editing, hypermedia, (a foundation stone of the Internet), multiple windows and on-screen video teleconferencing.

The majority of the demonstration centred round Engelbart using the computer to plan out a set of things that he had to do later. The list of things was organised, for example, as a graphical map of where he had to go, connected by the route he had to take. His shopping list was also organised hierarchically by category and he could easily expand or elide sections of the hierarchy or move items between sections.

Key to the human–computer interaction was the fact that the interface was intimately linked to the work environment and appropriate user-interface devices were used. His desk and workspace were built around the computer, which was the focus of attention.

This last aspect eventually found its way into the Macintosh and Microsoft Windows. The mother of all demos became the standard transition from an ordinary desk into a multi-dimensional, flexible, self-organised workspace.

Idea 50 – Great business idea? – Sell a piece of software to the entire world and keep charging for updates (Microsoft)

'Sir money, money, the most charming of all things; money, which will say more in one moment than the most elegant lover can in years. Perhaps you will say a man is not young; I answer he is rich. He is not genteel, handsome, witty, brave, good-humoured, but he is rich, rich, rich, rich, rich – that word contradicts everything you can say against him.'

Henry Fielding (1707–1754)

In 1977 Bill Gates' Microsoft sold a version of BASIC to Apple who marketed it as Applesoft. The flat fee for the software was $21,000, which seemed a good idea at the time. Apple proceeded to sell more than a million machines with BASIC built in, a fee to Microsoft of 2 cents per copy. No one can say that Bill Gates does not learn from his mistakes.

Microsoft has produced a lot of commercial firsts, including the Microsoft Mouse pointing device, but it was in 1983 that the big announcement came. Microsoft unveiled Windows, an extension of the operating system MS-DOS used by the grand majority of PC manufacturers and users. This graphical operating environment really would start to take the PC away from the boffins towards the mass user. In addition the company brought out Word and later made software available on the Apple Macintosh computer.

In 1985 the PC finally went graphical with the retailing of the Windows graphical environment. Market acceptance was slow due to the limited number of programs available. There were even some doubts as to whether Douglas Engelbart's vision of the user interface was going to catch on. They continued to develop the Windows concept and started to add usable software such as Excel spreadsheets.

By 1988 Microsoft was the biggest software supplier in the world and it had sold its millionth Mouse. And so it goes on, through Windows 2.0 to Windows 3.0, which was supported by a huge advertising campaign spend of over $10 million in six months. In return, Windows 3.0 sold 100,000 copies in two weeks.

1991 saw the continuation of a buying revolution. That year Microsoft shipped four million copies of Windows 3.0 to 24 countries in 12 languages. The momentum was kept going by PC manufacturers including Windows with their machines. The following year, Microsoft used television advertising to reach an even broader audience.

Windows NT took the company further into business computing, offering client server solutions. After a big build up Windows 95 was launched in August 1995 to nationwide interest. It sold more than one million copies during the first four days of retail availability in North America. By October that number had gone up to seven million worldwide.

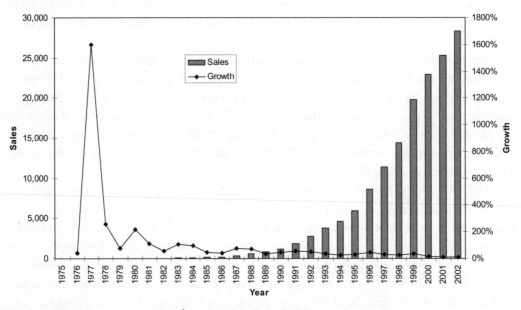

Fig. 1   Microsoft sales revenues ($m) and growth to 2002.

Internet Explorer became available to Windows 95 users free of charge, allowing many more people to use the Internet. The facts and figures never stop being phenomenal. There were 30 million Excel users in 1996.

Subsequent to this, Microsoft has produced and sold a plethora of software upgrades, from Windows 98 to Windows NT and Office 2000. It does seem that this idea still has terrific legs.

Perhaps the easiest way to describe this great business idea is to show a graph of sales revenues to date (Fig. 1).

Disregarding the 1977 growth rate, which distorts the numbers, the average growth per year is 60%. If this average continues, then the sales figures will look like Fig. 2. This predicts that in 2008 Microsoft's turnover will be more than $475 billion. To put that number into context, the UK Government's total spend for 2000 is approximately $620 billion.

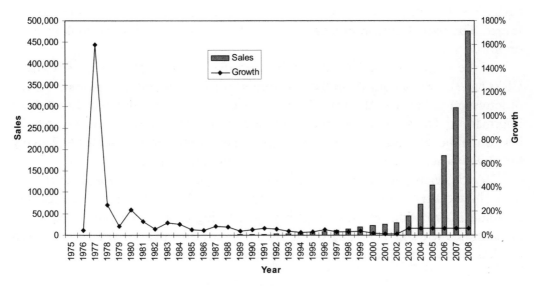

Fig. 2   Microsoft projected sales revenues to 2008 ($m).

Idea 51 – 'Our telephone answering system has broken down, this is a human being, how can I help you?'

In 1999 Barclays Bank in the UK announced that it was cutting 10% of the jobs in its branches and regional centres. One of the reasons given was that they intended by so doing to improve customer service. At first glance this looks unlikely, and the Bank's customers are still to be convinced. However, technology might just allow that apparent contradiction to be true.

For most utilities and finance organisations the high street shop or branch is giving way to the call centre.

The call centre may just be that unusual phenomenon – an improvement in customer service that also cuts costs and improves profitability. For most utilities and finance organisations, the high street shop or branch is giving way to the call centre.

At its best the call centre is more than a telephone answering service. It offers companies the opportunity to make contact with existing and prospective customers, resolve problems, promote products and make it easy for people to buy things. The basic function of a call centre is to retain customers and look for new ones.

At the heart of the call centre are the customer service representatives (CSRs). CSRs have access to data about their customers, their company and the many points of intersection between the two. They act as gatekeepers for the two-way flow of information. They are the intermediaries and interpreters. The technology is at its best when the mundane sorting and analysing tasks are done automatically, leaving the CSRs to handle the more difficult parts of the interaction.

Here is where the frustrations can occur. Interactive voice response (IVR) systems allow callers to serve themselves as far as possible. Customers have access to data and information by using their keypads. Using an IVR, customers have 24-hour service without troubling the CSRs. It's cost effective for the supplier and painless for the customer as long as everything is standard.

Where things go non-standard, or when the skills and knowledge of a CSR are required, a good IVR system will route the call to the person most likely to be able to help. It will also entertain you while you wait. The technology can also tell the caller how many people are in the queue and the approximate estimated waiting time. When the customer is put through, a link to the computer systems means that the CSR already has the details of the caller up on their screens before they start to talk.

As usual the quality of implementation of the idea is the measure of success or failure. Does the supplier provide a customer interface that is efficient and pleasant to use, or is a simple abrogation of the concept of service to frustrated customers.

On the other hand

If the call centre designers get it wrong, it can be the most frustrating experience ever, with the switch sending you from one message to another, until you end up back where you started. This is when you want to assist the telephone answering service to break down.

---

*F*ive *G*reatest *B*rands *E*ver

Introduction

There is nothing short term about good branding. The products may change, develop and become extinct – the original Coca-Cola contained two substances that you can nowadays be locked up for possessing – but the brand, with careful nurturing, remains. Most great brands tell consumers something about the product or service as well as something about themselves.

As usual, when talking of matters concerned with selling, the starting point is the market and consumers. You have to understand the needs and desires of the customer, understand the key attributes of the product and anticipate what needs to be done to relate the product to the values of the customer.

There is nothing short term about good branding.

Value is the other great starting point. Customers relate to products because they can relate to something in them that they value. The brand owner then communicates these values through every medium, through the packaging, the shop shelf, advertising, press comments and eventually word of mouth.

In the book *The Worlds Greatest Brands*, the editor Nicholas Kochan explains how the Interbrand (a branding consultancy) assessment of top brands works. These are the criteria and using a combination of them is how I have selected the five greatest brands ever.

- *Brand weight:* the influence or dominance that the brand has over its category or market (more than just market share)
- *Brand Length:* the stretch or extension that the brand has achieved in the past or is likely to achieve in the future (especially outside its original category)

- *Brand breadth:* the breadth of franchise that the brand has achieved, in terms of age spread, consumer types and international appeal
- *Brand depth:* the degree of commitment that the brand has achieved among its customer base and beyond; the proximity, the intimacy and the loyalty felt for the brand.

Idea 52 – Disney

You could say that the Disney company built its wholesome entertainment branding through the way it managed its people. Central to its success was the culture created by Walt himself – smart dress code, no swearing, and the use of euphemisms to describe the people who work there – 'cast members' rather than employees.

Then, through the generations, the company has used its rich catalogue of films and entertainment to merchandise its other products. So long as the movies are in peoples' minds merchandise can be sold.

The Walt Disney company also more or less invented the business of character merchandising – licensing other suppliers to use your brand. In character merchandising, the brand is usually represented by a character from literature, movies or television, such as Mickey Mouse. The brand is then used on products that are not directly linked to the character.

So, Mickey not only appears in films, books videos etc., but he is used to sell clothing, watches, toys, jewellery and even food. For example, until 2002 Nestlé has had the exclusive right to use Disney characters on branded food in Europe. Disney's earnings from this has topped $150 million, and all they had to do for this added profit was negotiate the contract. Everything else they were doing anyway.

They have been building the brand since 1928, and now have publishing interests, theme parks, movie studios, a mail-order business, hotels and a television channel. Their declared philosophy is to build 'an integrated system in which each Disney property enhances and reinforces the whole.'

It guards its brands tightly and is a wonderful example of the huge power of building brands on values and managing them well.

Idea 53 – McDonald's

Their managers sum up McDonald's as 'not just a product, it's an experience.' Surely the proof of the greatness of the brand is that it was amongst the first companies to expand quickly into Eastern Europe after the Berlin wall came down.

The brand means America, and an enjoyable lifestyle. Thus the brand has been built on cultural connection as well as commercial astuteness. It is a deceptively simple and universal formula – limited choice, quick service and clean restaurants. In short 'Do the simple things well.'

If the incursion into former communist countries is the big picture, then the narrower context of the explosion that is McDonald's is product and design consistency. With few exceptions – you can have a glass of wine with your burger in Paris, and the restaurant opposite Windsor Castle melds into its surroundings more than most – you do not know where you are in the world when you are in a McDonald's.

McDonald's does not have the branding completely solved. It is a highly centralised operation and it admits that it takes too long to get new ideas into the field. Both of these are difficult nuts to crack. The first requires a new way of motivating and empowering people, and the latter a faster cycle of listening to the customer and reacting.

Still, theirs is a big, global market. As McDonald's publicity bemoans, 'On any day, even as the market leader, McDonald's serves less than one per cent of the world's population.'

Come the start of the 21st century, McDonald's, though still a great brand, is showing its first signs of mortality. A huge price war with its competitors, and possibly the result of its difficulties in bringing forward new 'experiences' has raised questions about its future. Maybe McDonald's will end up as the greatest brand of all time for the shortest possible time.

But, the effect of the interiors, the concentration on families and children and the classless décor and appeal give the most truly international brand of them all. It knows no divides. For example, when Nato was bombing Serbia in 1999 both sides could eat McDonald's during the breaks.

Idea 54 – Coca-Cola

In a world growing more cynical, the values of freshness and naiveté seem to require re-examination.

Many people are expressing some concerns over the continuing viability of the essential Coca-Cola brand image. In a world growing more cynical, the values of freshness and naiveté seem to require re-examination. But the Atlanta management team have more than a century of experience to call on to steer this incredibly successful brand forward, and the central message 'Coca-Cola is a refreshing beverage with a great taste' needs no updating.

Coke's mission in the 1960s that the world should live by love and that Coke was the spirit of love, made a whole generation take the drink to its heart. Add to this the sheer embodiment of America that the red can with it's swirled Cs represents and one can see why the brand is distributed to more than 195 countries through an innovative bottling franchise system.

Over the years the company took its understanding that branding was more than packaging, but involved giving the product a personality, very seriously and has produced a breadth of branding unequalled. It crosses age boundaries as effort-lessly as it does national ones. This breadth reduces the threat to any brand of changes in local tastes, regulation, or political or financial stability.

The final word on Coca-Cola probably belongs to its consistency of advertis-ing. The contoured bottle was developed in 1915 and remains a part of current advertising, which features it against the equally famous 'red disk' logo. Overall Coca-Cola's global dominance shows no sign of slowing down despite pressures from its arch-rival Pepsi and the emergence of own-brand colas.

Idea 55 – Kodak

The story of the next greatest brand, Kodak, has one major difference from the previous two. Kodak has nurtured its brand not only on packaging, personality and advertising, but also on its technical ability to be innovative and stay ahead in product terms.

Once again the brand has been developed over more than 100 years, from its founder George Eastman's frequently ascribed quotation 'we have made the camera as convenient as the pencil.' But despite huge changes in the technology of the product, the consistency of packaging and advertising is again a striking part of the brand's success. The yellow packaging of its photographic and film materials along with its logo is as well-known as any.

But what of the word Kodak? The name was registered in 1888 and Eastman subsequently told how he created it. 'I knew a trade name must be short, vigorous, incapable of being misspelled to an extent which will destroy its identity and, in order to satisfy trademark laws, it must mean nothing. The letter K had been a favourite with me – it seemed a strong incisive sort of letter. Therefore, the word I wanted started with a K. Then it became a case of trying out a great number of combinations of letters that started and ended with K. The work "Kodak" is the result.' Sometimes great empires are built on genius being properly exercised and channelled.

From the first camera advertised with the slogan 'You push the button, we do the rest', through the immensely popular Brownie introduced in 1900, Kodak has progressed to become a world leader in imaging technology with manufacturing operations all over the world. It maintains its innovation with, for example, its development of photo CD in conjunction with N.V. Philips of the Netherlands.

Idea 56 – Gillette

You could say that Gillette has been at the cutting edge of marketing since it started selling its razors in 1903. Gillette scores very highly in the assessment of weight. This key component reflects its dominance over its particular market. But dominance must not hinder flexibility and speed of reaction to change. In the 1960s, rival Wilkinson Sword launched a stainless steel blade and Gillette responded very quickly for a massive company.

Today the brand serves as an umbrella under which the company markets a range of male toiletries. They have managed also to be successful with women as well with the first non-soap based shaving preparation for women – Gillette Satin Care for Women.

The brand continues with huge support and advertising including the slogan that went round the world 'The best a man can get'. The 2000s have seen further relaunch of the branded products – some with an easy-to-argue competitive edge, if you will excuse the pun, such as the Mach 3 razor. It has been widely applauded for its success in repositioning itself as a young dynamic brand despite its longevity. It is seen as in tune with New Man as well as Macho Man, the marketing equivalent of squaring the circle.

Here comes the twist

Take the brand characteristics – weight, length, breadth and depth – and test your brand.

---

*F*ive *G*reatest *L*ittle *O*ffice *H*elpers

Introduction

The office is a rapidly changing environment and always has been. Some new devices come into the office and seem to make things worse, others are so quickly internalised that you literally cannot remember how you did without them.

Here are some that seem, to most people asked, to do the job.

The office is a rapidly changing environment and always has been.

Idea 57 – Writing at ten thousand feet (Biro)

The inconvenience of having to dip a pen continuously to replenish its ink supply stimulated the invention of the fountain pen produced in the first place by the American inventor L.E. Waterman. The real breakthrough in convenience, though not necessarily legibility, was the development of the ball point pen.

Lazlo Biro, who of course gave his name to the whole genre, patented the first satisfactory model in the late nineteenth century. Biro noticed the type of ink used in newspaper printing presses dried quickly leaving the paper dry and smudge free. He decided to create a pen using the same ink. The thicker ink would not flow from a regular pen nib so Biro devised a new point by fitting his pen with a tiny ball bearing at its tip. As the pen moved along the paper, the ball rotated, picking up ink from the ink cartridge and leaving it on the paper. He patented the idea in 1938.

The breakthrough for Biro came when the British Royal Air Force bought the licensing rights to his pen. They needed a replacement for the fountain pen, which leaked when used at high altitude.

The US market was the real competitive battleground, with two companies, Reynolds and Eversharp, vying for dominance. On this occasion the war hurt both combatants due to quality problems and huge numbers of returns. Neither firm survived the price war, which saw prices going down from $12.50 to 50 cents. Parker Pens eventually sold 3.5 million 'jotters' in one year.

In the end BIC bought Watermans and sold pens at 29–69 cents. This highly popular version of Laszlo Biro's pen has daily sales of 14 million pens. It is hard to conceive of an office without this great little helper.

'No man was more foolish when he had not a pen in his hand, or more wise when he had.'

Samuel Johnson

Idea 58 – Clipping the oppressed

It is generally believed that the first known fastening of papers started in the thirteenth century when a short length of ribbon was placed through parallel incisions in the upper left hand corner of pages. This was followed by a seal-method, the act of connecting papers with wax and textile ribbons. Almost 600 years passed before any serious attempt was made to improve the ribbon fastener.

In 1835 a New York physician named John Ireland Howe designed and built the first truly practical machine for mass-producing solid head straight pins. In a relatively short time, straight pins were being sold by the half pound for the explicit purpose of temporarily fastening papers together.

On 15 March 1866 Johan Vaaler was born in Aurskog, Norway, north of Oslo. Even as a young man he was known as an innovator and inventor, and he graduated with a degree in electronics, science, and mathematics. He was employed by the owner of a local invention office where he invented the paper clip in 1899. Because Norway had no patent law at that time, it had to be approved in Germany to secure patent rights. Vaaler presented a number of designs.

It appears that his interest waned in following up on the German patent. Historians surmise that perhaps financial considerations kept him from doing more with his idea.

Across the ocean in the USA, a patent for the paper clip was awarded to Cornelius J. Brosnan of Springfield, Massachusetts in 1900. It was called the *Konaclip*. Gem Manufacturing Ltd of England followed with the first double-oval shaped standard clip. This familiar shape is still known as the Gem clip.

Several designs have followed these originals. Most failed to last, but some have remained. Those still manufactured today, beside the Gem, include the *Non-Skid*, which has small incisions cut along the length of the parallels, the *Ideal* pattern for holding a thick bundle of paper, and the *Owl*, named for its two eye-shaped circles. Owl clips did not get tangled with other clips, nor did they snatch at stray papers that didn't belong with the clipped stack.

There have been many unusual applications of the paper clip. During World War II, Norwegians were prohibited from wearing buttons imprinted with the Norwegian king's initials. Hence they fastened paper clips to show patriotism and irritate the Germans. Wearing a paper clip was often reason enough for arrest. They were a Norwegian invention whose original function was to bind together. They symbolised solidarity and opposition against the occupation.

Today a variety of uses exist, ranging from bookmark, money clip, and staple remover to the item that holds a hem that needs sewing or serves as a hanger for curtains, lights and pictures. Because of its price and availability, it is easy to see why the paper clip is one of the most versatile of inventions.

Idea 59 – From keeping your place to keeping your appointments (Post-It®)

Art Fry's inspiration for Post-it® Notes dates back to when he sang in his church choir in the early 1970s. He used scraps of paper to mark selections in his hymnal. Unfortunately, they kept falling out and he'd often lose his place. 'I needed a bookmark that would stay put, yet could easily be removed without damaging my hymnal', Fry says.

Art Fry realised his invention's full potential when he wrote a note on one of his new 'bookmarks' and attached it to a report he was forwarding to a colleague.

Around the time that Art Fry was thinking about how to make more co-operative bookmarks, his colleague, Dr Spencer Silver, was doing basic research on adhesives in 3M's Central Research Department. Spencer had created a low-tack adhesive that stuck lightly to many surfaces, yet remained sticky even after you repositioned it. Fry soon realised Spencer's adhesive was perfect for his needs. One morning, Fry applied some of the adhesive to the edge of a piece of paper. 'Now I had a bookmark that could stick to the page while exposing a part that wasn't sticky,' he says.

A short time later, Art Fry realised his invention's full potential, when he wrote a note on one of his new 'bookmarks' and attached it to a report he was forwarding to a colleague. 'That's when I came to the very exciting realisation that my sticky bookmark was actually a new way to communicate and organise information,' Fry says. Indeed, soon co-workers were at Art Fry's desk demanding more samples of his invention. The Post-it® Note, as we know it, was born.

It is not just little, yellow and square. If you look around your work area or home, you've probably got one, two (or ten!) Post-it® Notes stuck in various places to remind you to do something. Whether it's an ultra-coloured Post-it® Pop Up Note, handy Post-it® Fax Notes or decorative Post-it® Memo Cubes in a tropical fish design, you're sure to find the right note to suit your style. With over 29 different colours, 56 shapes, and 27 sizes, Post-it® Notes have certainly changed over the years, but one thing remains constant – they're great for reminding yourself, communicating and organising your thoughts, to-do lists and ideas.

Post-its have had detractors, people who when they first saw them were mystified, thought them profoundly stupid, unnecessary and expensive; in a word a scam. They probably buy them now in blocks of 64.

Idea 60 – E-mail

I know a sales director who watched, at first calmly, a reasonably heated discussion between two of his people who had a difference of opinion on the way forward for a part of their business. He watched through his e-mail, as each and every salvo that they fired at each other was copied to him. After a few days of this he took them both metaphorically by the ear and put them in a conference room with an instruction not to come out until the issue was resolved. Their desks were about twenty metres apart.

This downside of e-mail should not mask the glorious potential of global e-mail. Apart from the possibilities it raises for making money on the Internet [see *Four Greatest Ways (So Far) to Become a Millionaire on the Internet*], it is just possible that the political impact of e-mail will be as great if not greater than radio and television in terms of everyone having access to everyone all over the world. Dictators cannot like e-mail.

E-mail allows everything to happen simultaneously. As Oliver Freeman puts it, 'E-mail provides a sporting chance that globalisation will not be imperialism under a different name.'

Here comes the twist

When you come back to the office from holidays and find 1149 e-mails in your in-tray, don't just rave and delete them all knowing that the important ones will be followed up. Think through how you and your company are using e-mail and how it could be improved.

Idea 61 – Just give me the highlights

It is fashionable to describe current business people as 'living in the information age.' And there is no doubt that more information, or maybe I should say data, is available now than ever before. There's probably a number of fortunes to be made out of sorting all the Internet data into useable chunks, because the current search engines tend to leave surfers wading through the treacle of data trying to find the one fact they want.

Once you have it, either on the screen or in hard copy, the highlighter pen comes into its own, and it is my last nomination for greatest little office helpers. Everybody must have their quirks about where highlighters can most help them, so here is mine.

In the training and coaching of salespeople, role play has an important role to play. Managers or trainers should regularly exercise their salespeople by adopting the role of a customer whom the salesperson is shortly to meet. Salespeople don't much like it. They complain that they are much better with real customers than with role players. (Probably not true. The real difference is that most customers are too polite to tell a salesperson what they thought of a sales call at the end of it.)

To guard against the criticism that the role play is not like real life, the manager should have at his or her fingertips all the information a customer is likely to have. In fact their own briefing for the role must be extensive. So they lay out all the data on the desk in front with, of course, the key passages highlighted. Works every time.

*S*ix *G*reatest *M*anagement *T*hinkers

Introduction

Business spends a great deal of money every year on books, seminars and other ways of considering the views of the latest management thinkers. These people, particularly if they have an individualistic speaking style, become famous and sometimes very, very rich. But what of their impact on the actual running of the companies to whom they have sold their services?

Few of them have produced theories that have stood the test of time, even though their individual impact on managers who listen and adapt the way they do things is probably immense. I have chosen those whom I feel have changed how managers operate without necessarily being able to ascribe the thinking behind their actions to any particular guru. Such people can be said to have changed the environment in which people work.

Having made the selection we found an interesting common theme – it would seem that all the greatest thinkers and writers of books recognise that it is through people that things get done, and that their motivation and management is the crucial key.

Idea 62 – Douglas McGregor, *author of* The Human Side of Enterprise

It is often instructive when reading the annual report of companies to look at what they have said about their employees and search for inconsistencies. 'Our people are our greatest asset' is a good annual report cliché, often accompanied further into the report by how many of these 'assets' they have been able to lay off during the year's cost cutting exercises. The current scandal of directors' pay is another indication of inconsistency, where the pay rises in the boardroom are running at an average of 7–8%, leaving the employees' 3–4% looking second best.

And yet it must be better than it was, say, before the war. The culture change of how management thought about their people was expressed by Douglas McGregor in his book *The Human Side of Enterprise* (1960).

In this book McGregor invented theory X and theory Y as two distinct approaches to managing people. Theory X describes the traditional stick and carrot approach to managing built on what McGregor calls 'the mediocrity of the masses'. This theory regards workers as lazy and unmotivated, seeing their jobs as a necessary evil to earn the money to live.

The premises of theory X, McGregor writes, are:

'1 that the average human has an inherent dislike of work and will avoid it if he can
'2 that people, therefore need to be coerced, controlled, directed and threatened with punishment to get them to put forward adequate effort toward the organisation's ends
'3 that the typical human prefers to be directed, wants to avoid responsibility, has relatively little ambition and wants security above all.'

McGregor saw the implementation of this theory as a huge influence on the effectiveness of businesses. 'If there is a single assumption which pervades conventional organisational theory it is that authority is the central, indispensable means of managerial control.' He then goes on to show that theory X is not a reflection of the people being managed, but actually the result of the management mode itself. It is, so to speak, a self-fulfilling prophecy.

The other extreme is the theory Y company, whose assumptions are:

'1   that the expenditure of physical and mental effort in work is as natural as in play or rest – the typical human does not inherently dislike work

'2   that external control and threat of punishment are not the only means for bringing about effort toward a company's ends

'3   that commitment to objectives is a function of the rewards associated with their achievement – the most important of such rewards is the satisfaction of ego and can be the direct product of effort directed towards an organisation's purposes

'4   that the average human being learns, under the right conditions, not only to accept but to seek responsibility

'5   that the capacity to exercise a relatively high degree of imagination, ingenuity and creativity in the solution of organisational problems is widely, not narrowly, distributed in the organisation.'

McGregor was not so much known as a great academic but more as an advisor to practising managers. He was said to have the knack of taking behavioural science research and giving it sufficient resonance with managers to get them to put it into practice.

> *You know if the company is practising what it preaches by looking in at the shop floor, not by reading the section of the annual report on human resources and other assets.*

McGregor also examined the process of acquiring new skills and identified four kinds of learning relevant for managers: intellectual knowledge, manual skills, problem-solving skills and social interaction. The last one he claimed was outside the confines of conventional teaching. In his view, feedback on a person's performance or behaviour was more likely to occur behind the person's back than in a proper face-to-face discussion. McGregor advocated the use of T-groups to spread openness and discussion.

It is nowadays more than likely that senior managers believe that the values of their company are towards the theory Y end of the spectrum, and yet it is very difficult to operate wholly in that way. You know if the company is practising what it preaches by looking in at the shop floor, not by reading the section of the annual report on human resources and other assets.

Here comes the twist

- Examine all the attributes of a theory Y company carefully, and think whether your people would believe that that is how they are being managed.
- Try out giving face-to-face feedback to a member of staff whose behaviour is not satisfactory soon.

Idea 63 – Peter Drucker, author of The Practice of Management

'In most areas of intellectual life nobody can quite agree who is top dog. In management theory, however, there is no dispute. Peter Drucker has produced groundbreaking work in every aspect of the field.'
'Good guru guide', *Economist*, 25 December–7 January 1994.

If the assertion of the *Economist* is true, then many would say that *The Practice of Management* is the greatest management book of all time. It is certainly a book of huge range. It is based on much historical research and experience and for the humble management practitioner 'all human life is there'. Indeed one of the assertions of the book is that management and managers are at the epicentre of economic activity. So the book is important not only for the management process and practices it advocates, but also for the central role management plays in twentieth-century society.

Written in 1954, many of the theories discussed have survived the passage of time, and some have now been proven very prescient. He is never very far away from the first principles of business as he paints a picture of the nature and requirements of managers.

Starting from the heart of business life he says 'There is only one valid definition of business purpose: to create a customer. Markets are not created by God, nature or economic forces but by businessmen. The want they satisfy may have been felt by the customer before he was offered the means of satisfying it. It may indeed, like the want of food in a famine, have dominated the customer's life and filled all his waking moments. But it was a theoretical want before; only when the action of businessmen makes it an effective demand is there a customer, a market.' Such views are commonplace now, but they were originally propounded and tested by Drucker. This means that the only essential functions are marketing and innovation, a truth brought very much home to the people compiling this book of the greatest ideas.

From such philosophical beginnings, Drucker quickly gets to the specific practices required to run a thriving organisation:

'1 There must be high performance requirements; no condoning of poor or mediocre performance; and rewards must be based on performance.
'2 Each management job must be a rewarding job in itself rather than just a step on the promotion ladder.
'3 There must be a rational and just promotion system.
'4 Management needs a 'charter' spelling out clearly who has the power to make 'life-and-death' decisions affecting a manager; and there should always be some way for a manager to appeal to a higher court.
'5 In its appointments, management must demonstrate that it realises that integrity is the one absolute requirement of a manager, the one quality that he has to bring with him and cannot be expected to acquire later on.'

Probably the idea from *The Practice of Management* that was most seized and acted upon is the idea of management by objectives. It is interesting to note, in Drucker's description of this, the overlap with McGregor's *The Human Side of Enterprise*. Only a theory Y company could live by Drucker's statement 'A manager's job should be based on a task to be performed in order to attain the company's objectives … the manager should be directed and controlled by the objectives of performance rather than by his boss.'

While *The Practice of Management* has had its detractors, including a real trashing by Tom Peters, it speaks practically about, for example, the number of layers of management for any organisation never needing to exceed seven.

Turning to the manager of the future, writing over 40 years ago, we can see the prescience of the 'seven new tasks' for tomorrow's managers. They must:

'1   manage by objectives

'2   take more risks and for a longer period ahead

'3   be able to make strategic decisions

'4   be able to build an integrated team, each member of which is capable of managing and measuring his own performance and results, in relation to the common objectives

'5   be able to communicate information fast and clearly

'6   be able to see the business as a whole and to integrate his function with it – traditionally a manager has been expected to know one or more functions but this will no longer be enough

'7   be knowledgeable – traditionally a manager has been expected to know a few products or one industry – this, too, will no longer be enough.'

Drucker re-evaluated some of his conclusions later, but *The Practice of Management* was complete enough to act as the foundation for many of the developments in management thinking in subsequent years.

Ask yourself

- How much time are you going to spend today on creating a customer?
- How many of the seven new tasks are you confident about?

Idea 64 – Alfred P. Sloan, author of My Years with General Motors

It has always been well known to motorists that much of the financial value of a new car has disappeared as soon as it was driven off the garage forecourt; Sloan's strategy was that motorists should also realise that their brand new car was also out of date.

In the 1920s Ford dominated the emerging car market. Sixty per cent of the cars sold were Model Ts while General Motors could only manage 12. The received wisdom in this situation was that other manufacturers should concentrate on the much smaller luxury car market, with much lower volumes but potentially much higher profit margins. Sloan, on his appointment as chief executive, disagreed and aimed at the middle market with a range of cars that provided the car buying public with choice.

His next problem was how to manage a business of GM's size and historical organisation. The business had grown through acquisition of smaller businesses and no-one had managed to develop a corporate culture or strategy. Sloan was to build that, while at the same time allowing local managers to manage. More than 50 years ago he invented what have become known as profit centres or business units.

The divisions were made responsible for their market share and profitability, and given all the necessary functions to make them work more or less autonomously. There were five car manufacturing units and three divisions building components.

In a particularly forward-looking move, the component units were allowed to sell their products and services outside the GM organisation.

This 'federal decentralisation' was probably the first implementation in a company the size of GM. It set out to encourage the top executives to concentrate on strategy, leaving the operations side to the people at the front rather than to a remote, by style as well as location, head office.

On the other hand

Profit centre management can become counterproductive

A company, because it had got itself into serious financial problems, recruited a new managing director whose background was finance.

He rightly diagnosed the root of the problem as being in sales management. The sales managers were used to working with high gross margins and had developed expensive habits of discounting and providing free support.

They were not 'spending the company's money as though it were their own' and the company had become vulnerable to any slow-down of revenue. This threatened to cause further cash problems.

By Herculean effort the company's accountants produced the information and systems to push real profit centre management down to first line sales managers.

This lasted only for one year. The sales managers became totally introverted about their P&Ls and balance sheets. If, for example, a salesperson wanted to offer a trade-in of an old product to support a campaign to sell a new one, sales managers would spend a huge effort to unload the second-hand product on someone else's territory. If they failed to do so, the product was charged to their profit and loss account.

They would disallow sales in favour of making money in some other way.

It cannot be said that the year-long experiment did not work. Once the situation was made more standard by lifting the level of profit centres, the first line managers were much more conscious of selling profitably.

As became very obvious during the periods of trouble through which GM has had to go, Sloan worried about the problems associated with the company's size. 'In practically all our activities we seem to suffer from the inertia resulting from our great size' said Sloan in the 1930s. 'There are so many people involved and it requires such a tremendous effort to put something new into effect that a new idea is likely to be insignificant in comparison with the effort that it takes to put it across ... Sometimes I am almost forced to the conclusion that General Motors is so large and its inertia so great that it is impossible for us to be leaders.'

But prior to that in 1925 they had overtaken Ford. The new organisation and commitment to annual changes to its models had successfully put the good old Model T into second place. Sloan's segmentation of the market changed the structure of the car industry and provided a model for how firms could do the same in other industries.

Sloan's segmentation of the market changed the structure of the car industry and provided a model for how firms could do the same in other industries.

While remembered mainly for the product and organisational strategy, Sloan, it is interesting to note, again took a very lively interest in what we would now regard as progressive human resource management. Whilst he might from time to time miss out on policy meetings, he always attended personnel meetings and invested a lot of time in selecting the right people for the job.

Idea 65 – Robert Townsend, author of Up the Organisation

Some may find it odd to have the author of such a witty and irreverent book in a section dominated by the gurus of the century, but Townsend gets a lot of votes, and a reading of this book written 30 years ago shows that many of the points he was making were good enough to stand the test of time. It's just that he used hyperbole and wit to hammer his views home.

His starting point is that we all take ourselves and our businesses too seriously. The result of this is to constrain creativity and run the risk of trying to implement impossible strategies. He observes that 'top management (the board of directors) is supposed to be a tree full of owls – hooting when management heads into the wrong part of the forest. I'm still unpersuaded that they even know where the forest is.'

On the other hand

I wonder if this analogy was behind the later theory of bowling alley management. In this the middle managers are the ones bowling and senior managers the scorers. The twist is that senior managers erect a curtain through which the ball has to travel to strike the pins. Managers never, therefore, see the results of their actions.

The only feedback they get from the senior management scorers is to be told how many pins they missed.

But if you read the book twice – you miss too much the first time because of giggling – there is solid sense behind a lot of what is said. He hates the trappings of power, for example. His hit list in this area includes: reserved parking spaces, special quality stationary for the boss and his elite, muzak, bells and buzzers, company shrinks, outside directorships for the chief executive and the company plane.

Townsend's real claim to fame ought to be the fact that he was president of Avis when that company successfully challenged the market leader Hertz. Many of the tests of the organisation he suggests have been the subject of much effort by managers in the intervening years, but still cause the problems he identified. Here's an example in full.

'C: Call yourself up

'When you are off on a business trip or vacation pretend you're a customer. Telephone some part of your organisation and ask for help. You'll run into some real horror shows. Don't blow up and ask for name, rank and serial number – you're trying to correct not punish. If it happens on a call to the Dubuque office, just suggest to the manager (through channels, dummy) that he make a few test calls himself.

'Then try calling yourself up and see what indignities you've built into your own defences.'

But the people side is uppermost in Townsend's mind. (In fact he chooses McGregor's book *The Human Side of Enterprise* as one of the two best books he has read on the subject of 'getting things done through organisations'.)

Under *P for personnel* we get the succinct advice to fire the personnel department. His view is that they get in the way of managers hiring the people who they can work with. 'The important thing about hiring is the chemistry or the vibrations between boss and candidate: good, bad or not there at all.' Leaning too heavily on the personnel department is, in Townsend's view, an abdication of responsibility masquerading as delegation.

There is some truth in the observation that all presidents or chairmen eventually fail. If you keep managing a company the chances are that you will drop the ball at some point. If this is true, then Townsend's final chapter 'Wearing out your welcome' has a powerful force behind it.

'Nobody,' he writes, 'should be Chief Executive of anything for more than five or six years. By then he's stale, bored and utterly dependent on his own clichés – though they may have been revolutionary ideas when he first brought them to the office ... After five or six years a good Chief will have absorbed all the hostility he can take and his decisions will be reflecting a desire to avoid pain rather than to do what's right.'

If you keep managing a company the chances are that you will drop the ball at some point.

'Lesson for stockholders and directors: If the Chief Executive doesn't retire gracefully after five or six years – throw the rascal out.'

Perhaps his overall message comes through best with this: 'There is nothing fundamentally wrong with our country except the leaders of all our major organisations are operating on the wrong assumptions. We're in this mess because for the last two hundred years we have been using the Catholic Church and Caesar's legions as our patterns for creating organisations. And until the last forty or fifty years it made sense. The average churchgoer, soldier and factory worker was uneducated and dependent on orders from above. And authority carried considerable weight because disobedience brought the death penalty or its equivalent.'

In an article published in *Playboy* in 1970, Townsend ventured into the minefield of attitudes to women at work and the glass ceiling. His style does not change and his sympathy for working people shines through the hard hitting prose of 'The Guerrilla Guide for Working Women.'

He pulls no punches, as with:

'Q – Your job has grown to include occasional overnight travel. Your husband and kids feel this cuts into their time.

'A – Your husband is lying about how the kids feel. Ask them. Then ask yourself what makes your heart leap. Then divorce your husband or your job. Take into consideration that good jobs are scarce and men are a dime a dozen.'

Here comes the twist

Try the calling yourself up one.

Idea 66 – *Dale Carnegie, author of* How to Win Friends and Influence People

There are few more impressive sites in the world than a Scotsman on the make
J.M. Barrie (1860–1937)

The theme that runs through the four authors above turns out to be their emphasis on the people aspects of being a manager and a leader. It seems fair, therefore, to put this 1937 book in as the first self-help book aimed at improving the readers' skills in the people area. In Carnegie's recommendations you can see the documented foundations of all aspects of communications skills, from selling to solution selling and customer care.

Stuart Crainer, in his book *The Ultimate Business Library*, has Professor Hamel writing thus about Carnegie and the book.

'I recently attended a conference with the title "Implementing strategy through people". I asked the sponsor whether there was an alternative – perhaps one could implement strategy through dogs. When the focus is on technology, structure and process it is easy to lose sight of the deeply personal nature of management. Though Dale Carnegie's advice sometimes borders on the manipulative, it is a warm and fuzzy, eager salesman kind of manipulation. What a contrast to the hard-edged, got-you-by-the-paycheque manipulation familiar to thousands of anxiety-ridden survivors of corporate restructuring.'

When you read the advice Carnegie gives at the present time, you can be forgiven for wondering why he needed to do so much research and speak to so many people before being able to write the self-help book. This is actually a tribute to the fact that by now we have internalised or at least understood the principles that he describes. It is, after all, the only book title in this section that has become a cliché inside and also outside the business world. Here are the Carnegie principles in brief.

'The fundamental techniques in handling people' include 'don't criticise, condemn or complain; give honest and sincere appreciation; arouse in the person an eager want'.

Then he presents six ways to make people like you:

'1 become genuinely interested in other people
'2 smile [The World's Favourite Airline ran an entire change programme based round this]
'3 remember that a person's name is to that person the sweetest and most important sound in any language
'4 be a good listener [the start of most selling courses asks the question 'what is the greatest skill a salesman needs, and agrees finally on 'listening']
'5 encourage others to talk about themselves
'6 talk in terms of the other person's interest [advice in any training course concerned with communication]
'7 make the other person feel important – and do it sincerely.'

As Crainer says, 'Carnegie's message remains relevant: people matter and, in the world of business, how you manage and relate to people is the key to success.'

> **Ask yourself**
>
> Think of a key person you need to influence right now. Are you obeying all of the Carnegie principles as you seek to persuade?

Idea 67 – Tom Peters and Robert Waterman, authors of In Search of Excellence

It is unfortunate that this book is often remembered most for the fact that the excellent businesses that Peters and Waterman chose almost all made substantial mistakes later and lost their image as role models. However, the lessons drawn in this book have stood the test of time and it has sold more than six million copies.

The authors took research carried out when they were with McKinsey into what was different about excellent and successful companies. They got the list down to 62 including a number that you would expect to be there – IBM, Hewlett Packard and so on. They only examined big companies, but the messages and lessons they derived can act as a template for smaller organisations too.

The characteristics that they discovered in the chosen company were summarised into eight areas:

- *A bias for action.* Being proactive and looking for what needs to be done.
- *Close to the customer.* 'The excellent companies really are close to their customers. That's it. Other companies talk about it; excellent companies do it,' they say. They also have a suspicion of the too-smart managers. These are often MBAs who write impressive plans, develop and get their brains round huge spreadsheets (*Idea 48*) and have to hand 500-page market requirement documents. Sometimes such people are too clever for their own good. 'Our dumber

friends are different. They just don't understand why every customer cannot get personalised service, even in the potato chip business.'

- *Autonomy and entrepreneurship.* The excellent companies nurture such a culture throughout the workforce.
- *Productivity through people.* Here it is again. Peters and Waterman quote a GM worker laid off after 16 years making Pontiacs: 'I guess I was laid off because I made poor quality cars. But in 16 years, not once was I ever asked for a suggestion as to how to do my job better. Not once.'
- *Hands-on value driven.* The authors believe that the role of the CEO is to manage the values of the company. Executives in the excellent companies are not people who hire assistants to get things done, but are right there with their sleeves rolled up making things happen.
- *Stick to the knitting.* The successful companies are totally focused on what they have become good at and do not allow themselves ever to be distracted.
- *Simple form, lean staff.* They write 'One of the key attributes of the excellent companies is that they have realised the importance of keeping things simple despite overwhelming genuine pressures to complicate things.'
- *Simultaneous loose–tight properties.* This is probably the most difficult lesson to implement or even really understand. It started a lot of hares with people coming afterwards trying to put meat on these bones. Just how do you become loose and tight at the same time? How are managers controlled and empowered? How do you overcome the paradox of being big yet small?

What then is their legacy? The fame and success of the book spawned lots more academic and practical research and writing on the topics they discussed. The fact that so many of their excellent companies fell from grace should not stop us using their attributes at the time of their success as a template for excellence.

Ask yourself

How does your organisation measure up in the eight characteristics they described?

Epilogue

One final word on the 'people thing.' A manager attending the Wharton business school was interested to note the decisions his fellow students took when faced with the following dilemma. There was a conflict between two visiting gurus. One was offering a lecture concerned with the valuation of companies by looking at their cashflow, the other with a very people-related topic.

The students with little or no management experience tended to choose the finance talk while those with more experience all went to the people-oriented class. When asked which one he went to he replied, 'Oh the people thing, you can read the other stuff in books.'

*F*ive *G*reatest *E*nvironments for *P*roducing *M*oney *M*akers

Introduction

A cynical look at the business world quickly reveals that some environments in which businesses thrive are essentially a method of redirecting money derived from all taxpayers into the pockets of a few. *War Idea 72* is an inevitable and tragic generator of wealth and prosperity as are most political attempts to engineer a better or fairer society. Only the most fervent market forces promoter would deny that The *Common Agricultural Policy Idea 68* of the European Union had as its aim the solution to some real problems. These are faced by people working farms that are extraordinarily disparate by size and nature. Despite their differences they are trying to compete across national boundaries. Whole rafts of new questions are now being asked as the burden of the CAP hurts taxpayers, and through them politicians, more and more. But people make good, and sometimes easy, money out of it.

Religion too creates wealth on what some would say is a basic selling proposition of 'Pay up or go to hell.' For centuries the *Roman Catholic Church Idea 71* has built massive financial assets and other religions have done much the same. Religion also has what the city types would call a double whammy effect. It generates wealth in its own right, and generates more by being a major driver of wars.

Take-overs and junk bonds Idea 69 get a mixed press, and their desirability is probably more questioned now than previously, but could we do without them?

But first we take the *bête noire* of the Eurosceptic.

Idea 68 – Never mind the quality, pay the farmer

There is an apocryphal tale of a man living in the centre of a large town in Kansas who spotted a business opportunity. He planned to exploit the fact that farmers were being paid by the state for the same number of hogs they raised and sold last year, even though it suited everyone for them actually to cut down the number of hogs they brought to market this year.

Our man wrote to the State legislature in the following terms. 'I understand that you are paying people not to raise hogs. It has always been a business of interest to me, and I write to inform you that I intend starting a company not to raise hogs. This year I aim to start in a modest way and not raise just 100 hogs. Next year though I intend to build the business by at least double, and not raise 200 hogs. Who knows, I may need hired help.'

The Common Agricultural Policy attempts to regularise three types of agriculture present in the European Union. The first is the north-west plains. These are the most advanced agricultural areas in the world. They adapt to technology quickly, have highly trained producers and farmers and they possess significant capital. The second zone divides into two. The advantaged parts of the Mediterranean area, where a wide range of climatic conditions allows a reasonably high level of production, economy and income, and the disadvantaged areas such as the highlands, where the expenses of farming are much higher due to geographic and climatic conditions, and the difficulties faced in using machinery.

So go on. Decide what you do not want to grow or raise, write your business plan and claim your cheques.

In its attempts to regularise these areas the CAP spends some billions of pounds shoring up the incomes of agricultural workers in an environment where technology and efficiency is steadily reducing the whole value of the rural economy. The 6% of the working population who work on farms produce less than 3% of the GDP of the member states. This statistic may very well change as new countries join the EU in the next few years. They are also starting from farming economies and will need subsidies not to raise hogs just like everyone else.

So, go on. Decide what you do not want to grow or raise, write your business plan and claim your cheques.

Idea 69 – Take-overs and junk bonds

Take-overs could, of course, be in the section on winning in the stock market. It is usual for the shareholders of the company being taken over that they receive a premium on the share price once it becomes known that there is a predator, friendly or hostile, about. But there is a large body of opinion that believes that this effect is counteracted by the negative impact of the shareholders of the bidding company.

So the money makers in this environment seem to be the wheelers and dealers who make take-overs happen and who deal with the assets and debts of the company after the take-over.

Let's take as an example an American-style leveraged buyout (LBO) and see how the idea of companies being 'in play' has produced markets where a lot of money can be made and lost.

The LBO uses a target company's assets and earnings to finance the take-over. The buyer simply pledges the assets of the target company as security for lenders, who will only lend the money if the bid is successful. As soon as the purchase has been completed the debt is secured on the company's own assets. There are many examples, but one of the most famous was the bid for RJR Nabisco in 1989.

The result of all this is that the new company has the millstone of debt round its neck from day one. So, corporate raiders will sell off parts of the new company or its assets to try to get this more under control. This is called 'rationalisation' and is frequently attended by its close cousin 'downsizing'.

Leveraging is, whatever the junk bond salespeople tell us, dangerous. If the profits of the business do not grow to expectation or if interest rates take a turn up the way, trouble can ensue. The huge debts from the buyout may be the downfall of the company bought out.

LBOs are not so popular in the UK, although they too have a close cousin in the management buyout.

Normal company bonds are a well-accepted form of capital and carry a sensible degree of risk. In the leveraged situation the amount of debt involved makes the bonds themselves more risky. There is more risk, so the investors demand higher return, which makes things a little worse if all goes well, or a lot worse if the company's plans underperform.

'Junk bonds' is the term used to describe such bonds. Technically they are not rated as 'high quality' by the US bond rating agencies. A high proportion of bonds does not meet the stringent conditions demanded by these organisations.

So where there is a risk there is a market. Led by W.Braddock Hickman in the 1950s who showed that low-grade bonds would yield higher overall returns (even allowing for failures), Michael Milken (known as the Junk Bond King) popularised the idea and created the junk bond market.

Drexel Burnham Lambert, for whom Milken worked, promoted the idea of diversifying risk in the form of mutual funds and unit trusts, and for a while these proved successful in returning higher yield with reduced risk. The edifice went through a well publicised crisis caused, on the one hand, by allegations of insider dealing – Milken got ten years – and by a number of the companies so formed floundering. In the end a series of defaults on junk bonds left a trail of business failures culminating in the bankruptcy of Drexel itself.

Despite this infamous period, the high yield so-called junk bonds are still a permanent and important part of the global economy.

Idea 70 – Go on, devolve yourself

Politics is a great driver of business, and never more so than when politicians are, strictly in the nation's interest, spending money on, well, politics. The Scottish Parliament has announced its new executive of ministers and their juniors. It has a First Minister and ten other ministers in the executive, which is like saying of cabinet rank. After them come a further 11 deputies who report to the executive ministers. They all have salaries and cars. The Scottish Office in London has, in the past, operated with one cabinet minister and three or four ministers.

The total cost of the Scottish Parliament in a year is more than £10 million. As a Scot long domiciled in England I am enthusiastic about devolution of power to my native land. I am quite happy for there to be 22 ministers and a further 107 Members of the Scottish Parliament. There is, however, still a Secretary of State for Scotland and from where I sit the question is bound to arise – what on earth are they all doing?

Idea 71 – Please God, make me rich – oh, and let some of it trickle down to the poor

'His creed no parson ever knew
For this was still his 'simple plan'
To have with clergymen to do
As little as a Christian can.'

Sir Francis Doyle (1810–1888)

Religion probably has an equal only in war in giving rise to thousands of business opportunities. From the Egyptian temples and pyramids to the world-wide chain of mosques and churches, religion has given work to architects, builders, painters, icon manufacturers, musicians and every other trade and profession you can think of. It is a sobering thought that without religion Wren would have had to design workhouses and customs sheds. Without religion what would Michael Angelo have painted or what music would Handel have written?

Religion probably has an equal only in war in giving rise to thousands of business opportunities.

The main churches of the world have been mostly fabulously rich. You cannot easily find out how rich they are at the moment. The Vatican Bank, for example, still does not publish a profit and loss account or balance sheet.

The evangelists in America use television to bring money pouring in, on their simple unique selling proposition 'If you support us, we will support you in your bid to achieve immortality.' As long, says Pat Robertson, as you are not a homosexual or come from Scotland, which he describes as a 'dark land.'

Religious business opportunities arise also from inter-religious feuds. They have a habit of destroying each other's religious sites when they are at war or trying to rid their country of other religions. When and if the Serbs leave Kosovo, they are going to try to get Nato to agree that they can leave some of their troops behind for the task of guarding their religious sites.

This brings us logically to the next idea.

Idea 72 – War and the pieces

'To found a great Empire for the sole purpose of raising up a people of customers, may at first sight appear only a project for a nation of shopkeepers. It is, however, a project altogether unfit for a nation of shopkeepers; but extremely fit for a nation that is governed by shopkeepers.'

Adam Smith (1723–1790)

The impact of war on business is very profound. From the industrial opportunities involved in building weapons and ammunition to prepare for it, to the need for repair and rebuilding after it, there is really no equal.

The economics of war are bound up with the theory of late starters. Late starters are countries whose economies have gone through rapid growth later than others. The argument goes that they can leapfrog technologies and not only catch up but also outdo their competitors. In this century Italy, Germany and Japan incurred huge amounts of war damage and the late starter theory saw them building a new stock of capital incorporating the latest technologies. Indeed, the allies systematically dismantled and shipped to their countries the entire industrial base of Germany. This led to very rapid growth with the most modern plant and equipment.

The Allies might well have been better to leave the German machinery in place and build their own from scratch. This might have slowed the German miracle down a bit.

It is difficult to generalise about the beneficial impact of war on economies, so let us take a quick look towards the scene of one of the most recent wars – that in Kosovo and Serbia. Some of the missiles and 'smart' bombs used by Nato in prolonged bombing raids cost more than $1 million each and the stockpiles had to be replenished. A *Financial Times* estimate of the cost of fighting the air war was $7 billion. The same article suggests that the cost of the peacekeeping force in Kosovo will be more than the cost of the air war. Don't forget that, as wars go, this was quite a small one.

The bombs knocked out most of the river bridges in the country and a huge amount of other infrastructure. There were highly varied estimates at the time for the repair of this damage starting at $15 billion and going as high as $90 billion. Experience now suggests it will be nearer the former than the latter.

Whatever the bill is, many of the participating Nato countries supply the materials and expertise, and probably quite a lot of the labour to rebuild. The recent war in Croatia holds many parallels with the situation in Kosovo. German, Italian and French companies received contracts for building and other infrastructure work.

Britain sent a party of more than 30 companies accompanied by a trade minister to Croatia to get in on the act. Concrete was at a premium to rebuild the bridges and a British company built a cement plant in Split. The power companies in the UK and elsewhere took good advantage of the damage done to generating and distributing plant.

When Vegetius in the 4th century wrote 'Let him who desires peace, prepare for war' he could equally accurately have said 'Let him who wants economic growth, prepare for war.' Oh, and fight one from time to time.

At the time of writing the USA is building up a force of 250,000 personnel to fight a war in Iraq. The build up is costing billions and that is before they start to consume the consumables such as missiles and smart bombs. Just look at the statistics of the only American aircraft carrier in the Gulf by the end of 2002 – the 88,000-tonne *USS Constellation*, (The UK's biggest, the *Ark Royal*, is a mere 20,000 tonnes). The 'Connie' carries 5000 people, 72 combat aircraft and 30 different types of air-launched weapons. This includes the Slammer (stand-off land-attack missile – expanded response), which can choose its targets as it goes along, after it has been launched into the general direction of the enemy – $500,000 a pop.

It is also not just a job for fighters fit to be heroes; to fight the war in Iraq will require 1000 battle planners. So any type of person can get involved in a war, probably the greatest business idea of all time.

On the other hand

Wars have to be financed and generally that is done through increased taxation. In the USA, for instance, the importance of personal income tax as a source of revenues increased enormously during World War II. During that period they introduced higher tax rates, lower exemptions and deductions at source. At the same time the UK and many other of the belligerent nations resorted to a general sales tax.

Four Greatest Ways (So Far) to Become a Multi-Millionaire on the Internet

Introduction

The Internet itself must qualify as one of the greatest business ideas of all time. But it was, of course, to begin with an academic idea with the linking up of universities to allow each other to benefit from work they were all doing, so I have chosen its applications rather than the net itself. We have already looked at *e-mail Idea 60,* and in this section we look at people who have made vast sums of money by convincing people that they could hugely exploit the virtues of the net. Notice how they have not made vast sums by exploiting the net, but by persuading people that they were about to.

The Internet bubble of the late 1990s is a phenomenon widely written about, since it has had an impact on everyone's savings, pensions and economic success – and all of it adverse.

Perhaps the epitome of this phenomenon is Steve Case, the man who invented AOL and eventually sold it to Time Warner in 1999 with such good timing as to make one suspect he is a prophet as well as an innovator. The combination of technological expertise – AOL – with hugely successful content – Time Warner – looked to most people a real winner. Steve Case got incredibly rich; but it was just before the bubble burst. By early 2002 the shareholders, by now sitting on a share that had dropped 76% since the company was formed, got fed up. Wanting some short-term success as well as promises for the future, they outmanoeuvred Case and he left the company.

His, and some other peoples', vision still lives and the Internet is becoming more and more part of corporate and private life. To be fair, it was not their fault that a feeding frenzy started and professional investment managers decided they could not risk not joining the bandwagon and taxi drivers started giving share tips. This last is a sure sign of troubles ahead and, sure enough, all the companies involved have been revalued and many have gone out of business.

I have picked three applications of the Internet. One illustrates the real benefits that the Internet can offer companies in terms of building learning organisations – *Avoid the epitaph – 'They didn't follow through' Idea 73*; one that is becoming an important part of retail life and getting towards profitability – *Never mind high tech, there's still money in books Idea 74*; and one that illustrates the point that new technology requires us to think outside the square and look for ideas that are triggered from seemingly irrelevant events – *An Internet company built on a sweetie dispenser – what am I bid? Idea 75.*

Finally, lest we believe that we are cleverer than our forebears I have added the South Sea Bubble of the early 1700s to illustrate our current and continuing inability to learn from experience.

Idea 73 – Avoid the epitaph – 'They didn't follow through'

If you talk to consultants and trainers who work with large, medium and small companies, and get them to talk honestly about the impact their introduction of new business processes has had on their clients, they will talk in terms of the epitaph that forms the title of this idea – 'They simply did not follow through'. However enthusiastically people leaving training courses are determined to implement the ideas they have received, and no matter how sure management is that the consultant's report shows them the way ahead, the fact is that back at the ranch nothing has changed from the pressures that made all parties act in the way they were doing before. They leave off implementing the new idea while they get back onto an even keel and eventually they have forgotten so much about what they are supposed to do that the organisation becomes guilty of paying for some good ideas but never following through. If you don't believe me ask yourself how often you and your colleagues have taken training course manuals off the shelf they were put on when you got back to the office or workplace. Mostly they just gather dust.

A company called SofTools has developed a support platform that uses the Internet to help with this problem. Using the platform, trainers, for example, can convert their processes into electronic tools that sit within the platform. After the training course is done they can then act as online mentors, assisting their delegates to put into practice what they learned on the course.

The SofTools Integrated Performance Support System (iPSS) is a Web-based system that enables business teams to apply best-practice methods consistently – such as business planning, risk management, or critical decision-making.

The iPSS is seen as a 'virtual business coach' in that it will:

- teach the user about new techniques;
- provide interactive templates for completing the task;
- enable users to learn from each other and from the past; and
- give senior managers greater visibility and control across remote or virtual teams.

In the current economic climate, some would say that iPSSs are no longer optional for survival – they are a must-have. By licensing the iPSS to leading training and consulting companies, the platform is used to address a variety of key issues currently facing modern businesses: 'how to make the sales force more effective at planning campaigns', 'how to monitor and control operational projects', 'how to increase profit awareness at all levels of staff', and so on without limit.

The iPSS consists of:

- *Processes and tools* – structured templates reflecting client specific processes.
- *Online coach* – online self-paced learning environment – 'learning-at-the-point-of-doing'.
- *Experts* – access to the ideas and insights of internal experts.
- *Forum* – open discussion of ideas relating to projects, teams or competency areas.
- *Knowledgebase* – visibility and retrieval of real project or case files – both current and historic.
- *Portfolio status* – production of key management reports covering individual and team performance.

More and more consultants and trainers are seeking to make their training courses use new technology, but it is not until they could use such a platform as this that they have been able to do it quickly and at sensible cost.

The global availability of the experience of all the people in an organisation to each other will have many companies making money out of the Internet. Let's finish this idea with a simple example.

A sales force was trained in a new process for writing proposals. They went into a classroom for half a day and were introduced to the concepts of the new process. In the next two weeks they were asked to write one of their real-life proposals to the new standard. The expert who was teaching the process had access to their work and could prompt those who had not completed the exercise, first by e-mail and then by telephone. The number who completed the work was far higher than normal.

By the end of a series of training events there were some 50 real-life proposals on the company's intranet accessible through the iPSS. At around the same time, a salesperson found himself writing a proposal at 2 o'clock in the morning as it was due in by 10 o'clock that day (this is not an unusual scenario). He got to the point in the proposal process when he needed to describe the competitive edge that he believed his product had over the competition and wondered if any of his colleagues had produced a pithy and perhaps witty way of expressing this. By searching on the keyword of the product he was selling he found a number of previously written proposals on the iPSS and this gave him what he wanted. The sales director in this example is able to look at what people are proposing to write in their executive summaries in time, now, to be able to make suggestions for improvement.

Guess what? They are actually following through!

Idea 74 – Never mind high tech, there's still money in books (Amazon.com)

It is hard to argue with the quotation from a satisfied customer carried on the company's Web page, 'Amazon.com is an extraordinary company'. Martin Tanner, an

Amazon.com customer in Schoenenwerd in Switzerland, goes on to praise Amazon for 'doing business on the Web in a real customer-oriented way.'

Amazon opened its electronic doors in July of 1995 with a stated mission to use the Internet to offer products that educate, inform and inspire. They did this by offering an online store that is reasonably easy to navigate round and has a huge selection of books, CDs, audio books and computer games. In 2001 they served 25 million customer accounts, compared to 20 million in 2000 and 14 million in 1999. These customers are in more than 220 countries.

They have over 45,000 items in their electronic store, which they reckon is about seven times the selection you would find in a bi-box electronics store. They have millions of book on offer, some 200,000 of which can be browsed through their Look Inside the Book feature. Once again, they estimate a typical bookstore has 100,000 titles at any time.

The site gives the following services:

- Search for books by author, title, subject or keyword. For music, search by artist, CD title or song title.
- Browse for books in 28 subject areas or browse music styles.
- Get recommendations.
- Read reviews – either media reviews or reviews entered by other Amazon customers.
- See the bestseller charts.
- Stay up to date by getting Amazon to send you reviews of exceptional books in your area of interest.
- Buy gifts painlessly.
- You can even join the community by becoming an Amazon associate with the opportunity to earn money by selling books on your own Web site.

The founder of Amazon.com is Jeffrey Bezos. He had a finance background, being previously a Vice President of Bankers Trust Company and DE Shaw, a Wall Street investment firm.

It is plainly not relevant to value the company on its profits since it has none, but currently shareholders value it at something like 15 times its projected annual sales.

Bezos could not, of course, settle for being the leading online bookstore, and Amazon.com has moved into many other areas. Amazon.com Auctions gives its pre-registered customers the ability to buy and sell by auction items in more than 800 categories. With its service customers can not only bid easily for things but even have some insurance against the eventuality that the seller fails to deliver what the buyer thought he was getting.

Then they started to think of other things that could be sold in this way. 'No-one likes going to the drug-store' says Peter Neupert, the Chief Executive of drugstore.com. Amazon.com have invested in this online source for thousands of brand-name health and beauty products. Pets.com also attracted the company's attention with its popular and rare accessories, products and food for all sorts of animals.

Want to send a greeting to somebody who is on the Web? Use the Amazon.com free greeting card service with a huge choice of illustrations, pictures, animated cards and messages to choose from. If this seems a bit impersonal, you also have the ability to tailor the stock messages to suit your own preferences.

There is no doubt that many other markets are ripe for the Amazon approach. Huge markets in leisure, brokerage, cars, furniture, shoes and hardware are already online or on the way.

Luckily for Amazon they proved strong enough to survive the bursting of the Internet bubble and in the early part of this century are moving firmly towards profitability, with turnover in the third quarter of 2002 at $851 million and the quarterly loss down to $34 million.

Ask yourself

- Have you thought through how your products and services could be sold online?
- Check out the Amazon.com Web site to see the potential.

Idea 75 – An Internet company built on a sweetie dispenser – what am I bid? (eBay)

If you wanted to buy the company in question at the May 1999 share price you would have needed $24 billion. At that time, we were quite used to the fact that e-commerce-based ideas produced companies worth billions of dollars very shortly after they opened for business. But eBay Inc. did have one exception to the rules other Internet companies seemed to obey. It was already making money. In late 2002 they estimated their sales for that year would come in at between $1.17 and $1.18 billion. They have bought PayPal, the online payment company, and have remained profitable since 1999.

Pierre Omidyar got the idea from his wife, who was a keen collector of Pez containers. These are the little sweet containers made of plastic which dispense one sweet when you flick the top. They come in a great variety of designs and have for some time been collectible, in the same way, one could say, as cigarette cards were or phone cards are. Why could she not find fellow collectors on the Web?

eBay Inc. does have one exception to the rules other Internet companies seem to obey. It is already making money.

Pierre knew that people needed a central location to buy and sell unique items and to meet other users with similar interests. He set up eBay to meet this need and created the world's largest online trading community. It is, in effect, a new market entirely – one-to-one trading on an auction basis.

Individuals are the target users, not big businesses. There are now 1000 categories in antiques, coins, toys, stamps, jewellery and so on. In the words of the company's Web page, 'Users can find the unique and the interesting on eBay – everything from chintz china to chairs, teddy bears to trains and furniture to figurines.'

The reason for the success is the number of buyers and sellers eBay has managed to register. Plainly, buyers go where they feel they will get the most choice, and sellers where they think they will find the most buyers and therefore the best price. During the first quarter of 1999 the number of registered users went up by about 75% from 2.1 million to 3.8 million. This huge starting point made growth at eBay a self-fulfilling prophecy and, by 2002, the number of active users had risen to 24.2 million.

So, how does it work? Suppose you want to buy an antique Victorian pump organ, with bevelled mirrors, candelabra holders and Victorian stool. First of all you must be a registered user – a free process. This allows you to browse through all the antique Victorian pump organs with those attributes on sale (only kidding, the day I looked there was only one). You get to it through the category Antiques: Musical instruments.

Clicking on that item will give you the starting price or reserve and tell you whether or not it has been met. You are also told when the auction started and when it will end, the number of bids to date and where the article is. You can get a lot more information on the item and sometimes pictures, all of which have been entered by the seller.

Noting the bid increment, normally $10, you enter your bid. You are advised to enter the maximum you would pay for the item. This maximum amount is kept secret and eBay will bid on your behalf by increasing your bid by the increment number as necessary until your maximum is reached. You can, of course, review your bid along the way if your desire for the said organ reaches a higher pitch.

In common with the other Internet successes noted before, eBay spends a lot on advertising and promotion. There seems no way of short-cutting this expenditure. Indeed, it will be interesting to see if eBay can keep up its leadership as bigger companies get on to the bandwagon with much bigger resources, both financial and marketing.

So much for the past; analysts have predicted a bright future for eBay, forecasting $1.186 billion for 2002 and $1.83 billion for 2003. This is one company in the bubble that seems to be staying the pace.

One of the greatest business ideas proposed in this book, courtesy of Dale Carnegie, is the importance of listening. This includes listening to your partner when they want to expand the number of sweetie containers in their collection.

Here comes the twist

1 The Internet offers small and medium sized businesses the opportunity to play the big guys on more level ground. Even if it is just an advertisement, get yourself a Web page. Use it to generate interest, explain what you do and how well you do it and maybe get some e-mail enquiries. You can get software to help you do this yourself for a small outlay.

2 Once you have some experience of it, think about moving into online ordering and use the site more interactively. You may want some help to go to this stage.

3 Make sure that the site:
   • targets the right audience;
   • conveys the image you are seeking;
   • is consistent with other promotional material and your company's objectives;
   • contains content that is short, to the point, and it is easy for people to find their way round;
   • contains contact details on each page; and
   • avoids gimmicks and graphics if they make it a frustrating and time consuming task to download.

Idea 76 – The South Sea Bubble

The speculation mania that ruined many British investors in 1720 has no particular connection with making money out of the Internet, but it is a story which seems to fit quite well in this section.

The bubble centred on the fortunes of the South Sea Company founded in 1711 to trade, mainly in slaves, with Spanish America. The proposition was based on the company's expectation that the end of the war of Spanish Succession would signal a treaty to permit such trade.

The company's stock, with a guaranteed high interest rate of 6%, sold well, but the relevant treaty was less favourable than had been hoped. It imposed a tax on imported slaves and allowed only one ship each year for general trade.

The first voyage was moderately successful, but the real fillip to the share price of the company came from the confidence created by King George I agreeing to become the governor of the company. The lack of profits now, however, made loan capital to the company very expensive, reaching 100% per annum at one point.

In 1720 there was an incredible boom in South Sea stock as the result of the company's proposal to take over the national debt. The company expected to thrive in terms of growing trade, but the real profits were made in the value of the stock. The shares rose in January of that year from 128 to over 1000.

Overoptimistic company promoters inveigled a lot of people into a series of unwise investments. The market collapsed in December 1720 and many people were ruined. The share price returned to 120 and dragged many others with it. It also damaged the value of government stocks. The subsequent enquiry by the House of Commons uncovered a lot of fraud and corruption. At least three ministers had accepted bribes and speculated for themselves.

Obviously this criminal activity was an unusual feature in the collapse, but the situation reflects a truth about the underlying value of a company. The current share price of a business does reflect its future earnings stream, but if the gap between today's business performance and that expected in the future becomes too large, bubbles have a nasty habit of bursting.

'Behind every great fortune there is a crime.'

Honoré de Balzac (1799–1850)

Six Greatest Truths Your Independent Financial Adviser Might Not Have Told You

Idea 77 – Why are you in equities?

Building Societies are wonderful things – you give them the price of an overcoat and ten years later they give you back the price of a shirt. This means that you are forced to hedge against inflation by having some of your savings and a lot of your pension fund in equities.

Building Societies are wonderful things – you give them the price of an overcoat and ten years later they give you back the price of a shirt.

Idea 78 – Knowing how your investment is doing

Did your IFA tell you that the widespread belief that everything in business can be reduced to financial measures and recorded in the accounts is a myth fostered to continue to create work for accountants?

Idea 79 – Old but proud

Personal pensions are sold as essential vehicles for protecting your old age. In fact the combination of management charges, investment performance and scandalous annuity contracts means that most do not do this. Since despite saving thousands in such schemes you still live out your old age in poverty, the only benefit of personal pensions is that they give you the smug feeling that at least you tried.

Idea 80 – Keeping on track

Unit trusts that track the FTSE 100 index artificially inflate the share price of the biggest companies in the land, while ensuring that those dropping out of the FTSE 100 will find it very difficult to recover. This is very similar to the creation of the Premier League, which did the same thing for football clubs.

Idea 81 – Not so efficient savings

The efficient market is held to be true by the professionals. Since the efficient market hypothesis says that there is nothing a private investor can do to help themselves, they have to allow the professionals to earn huge commissions by churning their portfolios.

Idea 82 – Which Investment do you Trust?

In the late 1980s my wife did some work on understanding investment trusts as opposed to the unit trusts she had been used to buying. She raised this with our IFA. 'Why do you never recommend investment trusts? I have read of some good reasons why they can be expected to outperform unit trusts.' The reply was indirect, but made it clear that he would not be changing his policy.

Some weeks later he sent my wife a brochure for an investment trust. We wondered at this, until *the same day*, I read in the *Financial Times* of the first investment trust managers to offer sales commission to IFAs. You'll find it hard to believe that it was the very manager our IFA had changed his policy to recommend.

> 'Cecil Graham: What is a cynic?
> 'Lord Darlington: A man who knows the price of everything and the value of nothing.'
>
> Oscar Wilde (1854–1900)

*T*hree *G*reatest *N*atural *D*iscoveries that *D*rive *B*usinesses

Introduction

Three scientific developments have arguably been responsible for the highest number of business possibilities, outside energy sources such as oil and electricity. They are businesses on their own, but also make work and money in many related industries. *Explosives Idea 84* have many peaceful applications, but are also terribly important in the business opportunities opened up by *war Idea 72*. Another contributor to war, *radio Idea 85*, also enables all types of communication devices. These devices in their turn make possible the Internet, space travel, the television industry and many others.

But we start with a scientific phenomenon that leads to requirements for all sorts of professions and products. Because of it we need more police, a whole branch of criminal law prosecutions, a large percentage of the prison system, bouncers (big doormen), drying-out clinics, more hospitals, to name but a few. It is of course the discovery of fermentation.

Idea 83 – Fermentation

'O thou invisible spirit of wine! If thou hast no name to be known by, let us call thee devil.'

William Shakespeare (1564–1616)

What must the first person to discover the effect of fermented vegetation on his or her mind and feelings thought? How easy it must have been even at the earliest stage to trade such euphoria.

The origins of the business idea of fermenting vegetables and selling the results as alcoholic beverages, early on evil-tasting and later with a palate fit for experts, goes back to prehistory. The likelihood is that fermentation was discovered accidentally in pre-agricultural times. Early man clearly liked the effect if not the taste, and quickly moved to purposeful production. From merely gathering the raw materials which grew wild, he planted vines and other suitable crops.

Few products have been sold in such a flexible way to fit in with the rituals that accompany the drinking of alcohol.

Few products have been sold in such a flexible way to fit in with the rituals that accompany the drinking of alcohol. The traditions and regulations that surround the product have, on one hand, proved inhibiting to the sale and consumption of the product. On the other hand, from the earliest pre-literate times, alcohol was stitched into social ceremonies, particularly rites of passage, marriage and so on. A guaranteed market, with or without its potentially addictive nature.

There are records of the regulation of drinking houses in 1770 BC, and not much later beer and wine were popular prescriptions of Egyptian doctors.

The growth of alcohol consumption continued into classical times with an ebb and flow of what was regarded as an acceptable quantity to imbibe. From the Greco-Roman habits surrounding huge drinking binges in honour of the God Bacchus to the Judaic intertwining of religious ceremonial, which to the present day links drunkenness to irreverence and inappropriate behaviour.

The conditions of early societies foreshadowed those of complex societies including our highly industrialised one. Its role in a modern-day diet is largely irrelevant, with only the calorific value adding anything to the easy availability of other foods. As medicament it has a limited surviving place in tranquillising and pain killing. In religion alcohol has a symbolic role where it is not completely eliminated.

What remains is the satisfaction of personal and group needs, a breeding ground for advertising brilliance and long term marketing strategies of the highest order.

Alcohol consumption has gone steadily up since the 1950s and the market capitalisation of the UK drinks industry exceeds £65 billion, with combined sales of around £30 billion according to a spokesperson for the Wines and Spirits Association of Great Britain and Northern Ireland. These are very approximate figures.

Here comes the twist on the other hand

- There are changes occurring in the Inland Revenue's attitude to staff entertainment including the Christmas party. Few employees are going to see the joke if their attendance at the annual do is followed by an increase in their tax bill. Make sure you know what the rules are.
- There are various pieces of litigation both completed and pending, particularly in the USA, which deal with claims from employees and customers following accidents and other damage arising from drink obtained during company entertainment. Has someone in your company looked into this and checked your risks and liabilities.

If, however, you can still take a joke, you may be interested in a club formed by three Brits in a bar in Chicago called BOWFACE. This stands for 'Bars Of the World Found At Company Expense'. Members must have had a drink in at least three bars in at least seven countries in the preceding 12 months. Get in touch with the author if you think you qualify.

We have come a long way since the first primitive discovered the properties of mouldy vegetables, and millions of people have made a lot of money in the process. Funnily enough higher margins are made when governments are trying to regulate the product out of existence than in normal trading circumstances. See *Prohibition Idea 21.*

Idea 84 – Explosives

A multi-purpose product, explosives have a wide range of possibilities for making money. You can sell them as ammunition, the consumable of *war Idea 72*, as a method of blasting in mines and quarries, to build tunnels, or if all else fails to crack a safe.

One of the major quarrying companies in Australia, for example, has just placed a five-year contract for the supply of dynamite at a total price of $1 billion Australian.

'An explosive is any substance or device that can be made to produce a volume of rapidly expanding gas in an extremely brief period. There are three fundamental types: mechanical, nuclear and chemical.'

A mechanical explosion is the sort that occurs when a container is overloaded with compressed gas of some sort. This occurs more by accident than by application in the businesses mentioned above.

A nuclear explosion is one in which a huge amount of energy is released by sustaining nuclear reaction with almost instant rapidity.

Chemical reactions come in two types. Warriors use very large amounts of detonating or high explosive such as TNT or dynamite. The originating explosive, however, is the other type of chemical reaction – deflagrating or low explosives.

There is a strong case for the first use of black powder, a low explosive, being initiated by the Chinese although there are counter-claims favouring the Arabs. Originally used in China for fireworks and signals in the tenth century, it is likely that they moved quickly onto using it to make bombs. Certainly by 1300 the Arabs had invented the first real gun, a bamboo tube reinforced by iron to fire an arrow.

Use of explosives in engineering was, to begin with, a very dangerous business. Small quantities of black powder were lit in various containers, such as the goose quill. These were unreliable and burnt erratically. William Bickford, who lived in the tin-mining district of Cornwall, is credited with the invention of the safety fuse. The present day version is not much different from the original, which was a core of black powder covered in textiles such as jute yarn. The cord is covered with waterproof material such as asphalt and finished off with a layer of textile, or nowadays plastic.

Black powder is now illegal for use in mines in most countries and its use is declining rapidly. However, it still has no substitute for certain military purposes, and nothing equal to it has been found for making a safety fuse.

Ascanio Sobrero made the next big step forward when he discovered nitro-glycerine or blasting oil. This compound was so unstable and its detonation so unreliable that it remained more or less in the laboratory until the work of Immanuel Nobel and his son Alfred. They built plant for the manufacture of nitro-glycerine in Sweden and the USA. However, most experts believe that Nobel's invention of the blasting cap, a device for detonating explosives, was the next major step forward from black powder. Certainly the cap which Nobel created was still in use more than 50 years later.

There still remained the problem of the instability of nitro-glycerine until Nobel's second most important discovery. He found that by mixing pure nitro-glycerine with other substances, eventually known as dopes, he could render the nitro-glycerine stable and much easier to work with. Indeed he could vary the ratio of nitro-glycerine to dopes to produce an explosive that was not only more efficient but produced different strengths of explosion.

The military requirement for explosives has some differences to civil uses. They need to be insensitive to shock and friction and unlikely to be easily detonated with, for example, small-arms fire. They often have to withstand long periods of adverse storage without deteriorating, and must be fired in projectiles or dropped in aerial time bombs without premature explosion. Many types have hideously complicated, not to say devious, fuses for detonation.

These requirements are met in the main by trinitrotoluene or TNT. Indeed non-nuclear warheads still contain it as part of their chemical content, although there are some other specialist explosives in use.

There is an apocryphal story that emanated from the aerospace industry in the 1970s. It originated in the UK so it could well be put down to stereotyping and prejudice, but it went like this.

'Guided missiles have two main elements, the guidance system and the explosive. The difference between an American missile and a British one is the degree of expenditure and sophistication between these two elements. If a missile cost $1 million, the Americans would spend $750,000 on the explosive and the remainder on the guidance system. The British on the other hand would spend only $250,000 on the explosive leaving $750,000 for the guidance system.

'The effect of this was that the British missile would seek, for example, an enemy plane with pinpoint accuracy and get very close to the engine of the plane. In this case a relatively small "pop" would be enough to down the aircraft. The American type would get into roughly the same area as the aircraft and then a huge explosion would account for anything in the region.'

This only leaves the use of explosives in safe cracking. I can never forget the black humour of the film *Butch Cassidy and the Sundance Kid*. They too, on one occasion, overdid the use of explosives when they meant to blow open a safe that was being transported in a train, but actually blew the whole train into fragments causing a rainfall of the dollar bills in the safe.

Idea 85 – Radio

The number of products and services that owe their existence to radio must make the discovery of radio waves and the development of devices that operate with radio one of the greatest enablers of business.

Transmission and detection of communications signals, radio, consists of electromagnetic waves that travel through the air in a straight line or by deflection from the ionosphere or from a communications satellite.

The two significant characteristics of electromagnetic-wave motion are the physical length of the wave and the number of times the wave cycle is repeated in a given period of time.

Radio first became a possibility when the English physicist Michael Faraday demonstrated that an electrical current could produce a magnetic field. In 1864 James Clerk Maxwell, a professor of experimental physics at Cambridge, proved mathematically that these electrical disturbances could be detected at considerable distances. Maxwell predicted that this electromagnetic energy could move outward in waves, travelling at the speed of light. In 1888 Heinrich Hertz demonstrated that Maxwell's prediction was true for transmissions over short distances.

At this point the Italian physicist Marconi perfected a radio system that in 1901 transmitted Morse code over the Atlantic Ocean. Next came the development of the vacuum tube, which amplified or strengthened the radio signal that was received at an antenna; thus, much weaker signals could be transmitted and received than had previously been possible.

It was next discovered that the electric current in a vacuum tube could be made to oscillate. An electric-tube oscillator was thus able to generate very pure radio waves. Reception was improved with the refining of the tuning circuit. These and other components needed to produce radio receivers of acceptable quality underwent rapid improvement in the period before World War II.

Individual broadcasting stations were assigned a portion of an arbitrary frequency scale, so that the signal of one station would not interfere with each other. Other frequency ranges have been reserved for the many additional uses of radio signals, which include navigational aids for ships and aircraft, two way voice transmission, and space and satellite communications.

Innovations after the war, especially the replacement of tubes by transistors and of wires by printed circuits, drastically reduced the amount of power the receiver needed to operate and allowed its components to be miniaturised. Other advances included improvements in the sound fidelity of transmitting and receiving equipment and the perfection of FM stereo broadcasting.

But the real and outstanding benefit of all time that radio brought were the dialogues between the two chorus boys in the radio programme *Round the Horne*. They did odd jobs for Kenneth Horne when they were between engagements, and their opening went 'Hallo, I'm Julian and this is my friend Sandy.' Thank you Mr Faraday.

*F*our *G*reatest *B*reakthroughs *M*ade by *A*dvertising

Introduction

I picked advertising campaigns more from what we can learn from them, rather than for the brilliant creative leap that makes an ad or a slogan stand out. Such brainwaves occur from time to time, but tend to be the end product of a lot of research and work. It is illustrations of that work and the calculation of the results of campaigns that have dictated the choice.

A breakthrough occurs when a minnow attacks a well-established player, for example *Knorr Idea 88*, or when an ad has a result disproportionate to the subtle change in presentation such as *Alka-Seltzer Idea 87*. Since we are looking for relevance to current business people, the ads tend to be near to the present time.

Ask yourself

1 Check your advertising against the criteria posed by Roderick White:
  - Does the ad make me stop and read it?
  - Is there an original unusual idea in it?
  - Does it work as a piece of design?
  - Is it easy to understand?

---

2 Check the critical questions specific to the ad:
- Does this advertisement fit the strategy?
- Will it work?

Idea 86 – Correcting a myth (Kellogg's)

Here is an example of a great business idea from the 1980s. From the middle of the decade, Kellogg's All-Bran had a problem. Although consumers still recognised the benefits of fibre, they were switching from All-Bran to tastier foods, which they felt contained as much fibre as All-Bran but were more exciting to eat.

An ad campaign was designed to address this by concentrating on the fact that All-Bran contains more fibre than most of the other foods that people perceive as being rich in fibre. For example, a single bowl of All-Bran contains as much fibre as nine slices of brown bread.

The voice over of the ad went 'It's a fact that nine out of ten people still aren't eating enough fibre. So it's worth knowing that in every bowl of Kellogg's All-Bran there's about as much fibre as you'd find in nine nutritious slices of brown bread.'

The visual background to this is a hand putting the second slice of brown bread into a toaster. The toaster eventually pops and nine slices of bread leap into the air. The camera follows the toast then cuts to an empty cereal bowl beside a packet of Kellogg's All-Bran. The nine slices then land in the bowl and the frame is frozen.

Volumes, according to Kellogg's, which were declining at the rate of about 10% per annum, increased by 8% in 1990 and 14% in 1991, the two years following this great idea.

Idea 87 – Double doses (Alka-Seltzer)

The Austrian psychologist Herta Herzog was working for the Jack Tinker agency in

New York City in the 1970s. She suggested to her client Alka-Seltzer that the photographs in advertisements should show a hand dropping two tablets into a glass instead of one. They doubled their sales.

Idea 88 – Taking on a beefy adversary (Knorr)

When attacking a market leader, you do not have to go for the whole global market. Sometimes a little local campaign can make the difference. Particularly if you combine it with the theme that runs through good advertising practice. 'Listen to and know your market.'

About 20 years after launching its competitor to the Oxo Cube, Knorr had made some progress. It had 7.8% of the UK cube market compared to the dominating 89.6% of the leader. The characteristics of the products the two companies produced had significant differences. Knorr produced a more subtle flavour. It tended to enhance the taste of food rather than, as was the case with Oxo, dominate the flavour. This led in turn to Oxo being 88% of the beef cube market but only 12% of the chicken, compared with Knorr's 58%.

The situation was also different in Scotland, where Knorr had about a third of sales and Oxo two-thirds. The marketers investigated this difference and put it down to the Scottish habit of making home-made soups. Research showed that only 25% of home-made soup in Scotland had a cube in it at all. The cooks did not know that a cube could produce the same flavour as real stock.

Knorr took a decision to tackle the local market and encourage the making of soup and the use of its more subtle flavouring to act as the stock component.

BMP produced a creative idea called 'Monday Night'. This centred on two friends in the Scottish Highlands. They were cooking blind, and Hughie assumed that, since Sunday had been chicken, Monday night would be chicken soup. Wifey back home then surprised him with pea and ham. Her secret? Knorr Ham Stock cubes.

There were various updates to the formula over the 15 years of the campaign. The wife's appearance changed for example and the wit became more trenchant. In one ad the men were eating cock-a-leekie soup and mourning the death of Moira, the chicken they decided had gone into the pot to make the soup. The chicken then turned up – Voice Over: 'Knorr Stock cubes – good soup and no bones about it'.

Sales of Knorr cubes grew steadily over the years to become the brand leader in Scotland. Almost as important was the fact that the growth was indeed based on changes in soup making behaviour, which it was believed would not have occurred without the campaign. Because the Knorr cubes sold at a premium to Oxo, the share by value was two-thirds to Knorr. They became a £4 million brand compared with Oxo's £2 million.

So, a global brand can be encouraged in suitable local circumstances.

Idea 89 – If the logic isn't compelling, tug the heartstrings (BT)

As the modernisation of its telephone exchanges spread, BT had many opportunities to encourage the use of the advanced facilities the new equipment made possible. Test mailings of new facilities had convinced the company that a single-minded approach was more effective than announcing a raft of possibilities at the same time.

One such opportunity was Call Waiting, the giving of a signal to a person on the phone showing that someone else was trying to contact them.

Interest in the service when promoted rationally was limited. People found it difficult to imagine a personal call that was important enough for them to interrupt the call they were already on. Vitally important calls were felt to be rare, and callers who got the engaged signal were expected to try again. These objections disappeared when the communication promoted an emotional benefit rather than a rational one. At the time of trying out concepts, the scenario that most persuaded customers of the need for the service showed a girl in a phone box outside a station on a dark wet night trying to call her parents.

A campaign was launched, aimed at the parents of teenage children. The creative executions simply depicted people in miserable situations trying to get through on the phone, a boy who had lost his bus pass failing to attract the attention of his parents because his teenage sister was catching up on the gossip, and so on. The advertising was in the press and on the radio. It was timed to precede a mailshot. From a London testing it was seen to work well and was rolled out. BT recovered the direct costs of the campaign from revenues within 18 months.

If you can do it for call waiting, you can probably tug the heartstrings for just about anything.

If you can do it for call waiting, you can probably tug the heartstrings for just about anything.

Ten Greatest Ideas that Do Not Fit a Pattern

Idea 90 – Membership of a broad church

If you join any one club, you commonly gain the benefits of their associate relationships with other clubs. Clubman's Club gave associate membership of a multitude of clubs all around the world. At a time when people were travelling more and more for business it was a huge success and the inventors made a lot of money.

Idea 91 – Use someone else's storage space (Toyota)

Toyota were very short of inventory space at one of their plants. The site was so restricted that they did not have room to extend the warehouse. So, they invented and sold to their suppliers the concept of Just in Time. This meant that the components arrived from suppliers just before they were needed in the assembly area. This considerably reduced Toyota's need for storage space.

The idea caught on and manufacturers forced their suppliers to revamp their distribution and computer systems in order to comply with the strict rules of delivery. There were many examples of suppliers struggling to comply, and having to put in makeshift, and sometimes expensive, solutions to their customers' demands. So scared were the suppliers of failing, that solutions included having the next batch for delivery sitting round the corner from the manufacturer in the supplier's delivery lorries until the just in time order came.

Idea 92 – Getting productivity through job security? (IBM)

In the depression IBM decided to maintain its prime objective of offering secure employment. So at a time when competitors were contracting, IBM grew as new products and markets simply had to be found. They found that productivity stayed high, since, unlike almost everyone else during this period, employees were not afraid that they would work themselves out of a job.

> *'The average IBM'r has lost sight of the reasons for his company's existence. IBM exists to provide a return on invested capital to the stockholders.'*
>
> John Akers (b. 1934)

Idea 93 – Come on, customers, put your back into it

The process of self-service, which has revolutionised petrol station forecourts and supermarkets, involves the spectre of price cuts, normally not conducive to good margins. But the cuts are in effect value transfers from the supplier to the customer, riding on the back of the customer's forced labour. This may seem odd, but actually lines up with the need for speed and control even if you are being exploited at the same time.

Idea 94 – Improve the packaging, improve the sales

In the world of books the invention of the illustrated paperback cover proved that paperbacks need not look like cheap editions after all. This breakthrough was credited to Joe Pacey of Panther Books in the 1950s. It broke Penguin's stranglehold on the word paperback and signalled the final curtain for the popular hardback.

Idea 95 – Bring to market something newsworthy

Perhaps the greatest amount of unpaid-for advertising ever is that gained by the drug Viagra. This is a cure for male and, would you believe, possibly female, impotence. There is no doubt that it meets a growing need and that men who hitherto did not bother their doctor with an embarrassing problem are flocking to pick up prescriptions.

For a while no day went by without the drug being mentioned in the quality as well as red-top press. Not many products have received this much Parliamentary time, nor inspired so many interviews and discussions. MPs even discussed the threat of people using Viagra as a recreational drug. Probably no-one had thought of that before. Pharmaceuticals have spawned many great business ideas and free advertising, but I think Viagra will be the one that something gets erected for.

Idea 96 – Make it so that customers can always be on the phone

There is a new phenomenon on the platforms of railway stations now. It is a businessman or woman carrying a laptop in one hand and a brief case in the other. And yet they are still on the phone. By using an earpiece and a small microphone they can make calls hands free. This must be the dream of the phone companies.

On the other hand

Some would say that mobile phones persuade executives that it is easier to leave a mobile phone number than it is to train and empower their staff to make decisions in their absence. See the human resources advice in Greatest Management Thinkers.

Idea 97 – Set a thief to catch a thief

A great business innovation was to appoint Joseph P. Kennedy as the first head of the US Securities and Exchanges Commission. It had two benefits. It took Kennedy, probably the biggest conman in the history of the modern stock market, off the streets, and put someone who really understood stock fraud in charge of writing the rules.

Idea 98 – Make the real money on the side

A little time ago I had to change the printer that I attach to my laptop. The main criterion was that its weight and bulk should allow me to carry it around easily. I remembered that the original one, which had eventually gone wrong, cost £200 some three years previously and was expecting a good reduction in price. In fact they were still the same price but for £200 you could now get a colour printer. Quite impressive.

At the check out I was given the hard-sell by two assistants who tried to sell me an extended warranty contract to cover years two and three of the printer's life. Being a sucker for a salesman I bought it. It cost £50 and was almost certainly where the retailer made the real money.

Similarly pubs, originally designed to make money out of drinks, now make the real profits from food. Packaged holiday companies have wafer-thin margins on the holiday itself but do well out of selling holiday insurance. And so it goes on.

The principle is simple. Use the core business to cover your costs and make the cream on the top with other products, which can be cross-sold.

Ask yourself

Does such an idea have relevance in your business?

Idea 99 – Know your risks

There is a major parade taking place right through central London and some 25,000 people are expected to come to watch it. You have an opportunity to buy one of the concessions. If you buy the ice-cream concession and it is a nice day you will clean up. If you buy the umbrella concession, you will make a fortune if it rains.

There is an alternative to this high risk/high return decision. You could go in with someone else and effectively own half of each concession. You are bound to make money, but nothing like the fortune you would have made had climatic conditions suited you.

You pays your money and you takes your risks.

Idea 100 – Its up to you

There is no idea 100. It is almost certain that in this compilation I have missed your all-time favourite, brilliant business idea of all time. So this is your opportunity.

Write the idea, or as many ideas as you wish in this blank space, tear it out and send it to the author or the publishers (addresses at the front). There's a bottle of champagne for the best ideas, and if we get enough responses we will be able to publish a sequel – *The Next Hundred*. Now that's a great idea.

Contributors of Ideas

I am grateful to all the people who contributed ideas, from the obvious to the brilliant, from the merely creative to the truly bizarre:

Philip Allin
Penny Ariff
Philip Blackwell
Alan Bonham
Andrew Campbell
Stephan Chambers
Andy Davies
Oliver Freeman
Diana Hall
Gwyn Headley
Glenis Humphreys
Richard Humphreys
Chris Kerr
Art Kleiner
Alex Lajoux
Kate Langdon
Dean LeBaron
Graham Mackenzie-Washington (winner of the bottle of champagne).

Contributors of Ideas

*P*ublications *C*onsulted

Advertising – What It Is and What It Does, Roderick White, McGraw Hill, 1993

Amazon.com

Amway Web page

Ann Summers publicity and Web page

Avon Web page

Camelot Web page and annual accounts

Dell Web page and literature

Encyclopaedia Britannica

Eurotunnel Web page

Farepak Plc

First Direct publicity material

Forbes, global, March 22 1999

Forbes, global, May 17 1999

Honda Web page

IT Management Handbook, Edited by Rob Dixon and Ray Franks, Butterworth Heinemann, 1992

Kleeneze Web page

Liar's Poker, Michael Lewis, Hodder and Stoughton, 1989

Mousesite Web page

Post-it Web page

Premier Technologies Web page

Prudential Assurance Company Web page

Royal Mint publicity material

Sears Web page

Smart Things to Know about Strategy, Richard Koch, Capstone, 1999

Station X, Michael Smith, Channel 4 Books, 1998

Strategy Pure and Simple: How Winning CEOs Outthink Their Competition, Michel Roberts, McGraw Hill, 1997

Successful Personal Investing, published by Independent Research Services (continuously)

The Agricultural Structure of the European Union, EU, 1998

The Enigma of Intelligence, Andrew Hodges, Unwin Paperbacks, 1985

The Ultimate Business Library, Stuart Crainer, Capstone, 1998

The World's Greatest Brands, edited by Nicholas Kochan, Interbrand, 1997

Trivial Pursuit Web page

Vodafone Web page

Appendices

Appendix 1 – Answers to Idea 38

1   MDCCLXXXXV
2   CLXXXXVII
3   MMMCCCLXVI

Appendix 2 – Example for Idea 43: holding BP shares

	Investment record						Feb May				
Name of company					Usual date of interim dividend		Feb May				
Type of share		Year ends _____			Usual date of final dividend		Aug Nov				

Date	Number of shares bought	Balance held	Month cost	Dividends	Proceeds from sales	Mid price per share	Selling price	Net selling value	Monthly c/f	DCF	Annualised
September 1995		0					£0.00	£0.00	£0.00		
October 1995		0					£0.00	£0.00	£0.00		
November 1995	284	284	1346.16				£0.00	£0.00	-£1,346.16		
December 1995		284					£0.00	£0.00	£0.00		
January 1996		284					£0.00	£0.00	£11.36		
February 1996		284		£11.36			£0.00	£0.00	£0.00		
March 1996		284					£0.00	£0.00	£0.00		
April 1996		284					£0.00	£0.00	£0.00		
May 1996		284		£12.07			£0.00	£0.00	£12.07		
June 1996		284					£0.00	£0.00	£0.00		
July 1996		284					£0.00	£0.00	£0.00		
August 1996		284		£12.07			£0.00	£0.00	£12.07		
September 1996		284					£0.00	£0.00	£0.00		
October 1996		284					£0.00	£0.00	£0.00		
November 1996		284		£14.20			£0.00	£0.00	£14.20		
December 1996		284					£0.00	£0.00	£0.00		
January 1997		284					£0.00	£0.00	£0.00		
February 1997		284		£14.20			£0.00	£0.00	£14.20		
March 1997		284					£0.00	£0.00	£0.00		
April 1997		284					£0.00	£0.00	£0.00		
May 1997		284					£0.00	£0.00	£0.00		
June 1997		284					£0.00	£0.00	£0.00		
July 1997		284					£0.00	£0.00	£0.00		
August 1997		284		£14.91			£0.00	£0.00	£14.91		
September 1997		284					£0.00	£0.00	£0.00		
October 1997		284					£0.00	£0.00	£0.00		
November 1997	2	286		£0.77			£0.00	£0.00	£0.77		
December 1997		286					£0.00	£0.00	£0.00		
January 1998	246	532	2039.98				£0.00	£0.00	-£2,039.98		
February 1998	2	534		£3.19			£0.00	£0.00	£3.19		
March 1998		534					£0.00	£0.00	£0.00		
April 1998		534					£0.00	£0.00	£0.00		
May 1998	4	538		£2.42			£0.00	£0.00	£2.42		
June 1998		538					£0.00	£0.00	£0.00		
July 1998		538				£8.75	£8.53	£4,589.81	£4,589.81	1.87%	24.86%
August 1998		538					£0.00	£0.00	£0.00		
July 2001		538					£0.00	£0.00	£0.00		
August 2001		538					£0.00	£0.00	£0.00		
September 2001		538					£0.00	£0.00	£0.00		
October 2001		538					£0.00	£0.00	£0.00		
Total											24.86%

Index